"Like living beings, monasteries se _____ physical characteristics, and perso_ _____ _____ _____ a unique blending of history, geography, struggle, and chance, along with the myriad influences of the people over the decades who walked through their doors. Mount Angel Abbey has a compelling story to tell, propelled by the fullness of its long life. Father Joel Rippinger's novelistic telling of that story gives this monastery the care and attention it deserves."

—Judith Valente, OblSB, author of *How To Live: What The Rule of St. Benedict Teaches Us About Happiness, Meaning and Community; Atchison Blue: A Search for Silence, A Spiritual Home and A Living Faith;* and *The Art of Pausing*

"Fr. Joel has condensed 140 years of Mount Angel Abbey's history into a well-constructed 190-page narrative. He situates the abbey's story in the political and religious history of Europe and North America. He has made very good use of monastic archives. I hope that his work inspires others to tell us more about the personalities and the material and spiritual history of this fascinating community."

—Fr. Hugh Feiss, OSB
Monastery of the Ascension, editor of *A Benedictine Reader: 530–1530*

"Rippinger's book is a welcome contribution to the story of American Catholicism and American Benedictine history in particular. With a keen historical sense and deftness of narrative style, the author tells the story of one monastery's faith-filled journey—the story of a community of men sometimes imperfect and broken, yet intrepid in their search for God, the pursuit of holiness, and service to the church. Mount Angel Abbey's story is not theirs alone. It belongs to the church and bears witness to the truth that transfiguration does not happen without risk and hope-filled perseverance. *Struggle and Ascent* is a work that affirms the 'good news' of how God works in the church and in the world."

—Ephrem Hollermann, OSB, author of *The Reshaping of a Tradition: American Benedictine Women, 1852–1881*

"Fr. Joel Rippinger's latest contribution to American monastic history, *Struggle and Ascent: The History of Mount Angel Abbey*, presents a fascinating story in an engaging style. He situates well the 140–year history of the oldest Benedictine Abbey west of the Rockies within the context of both the history of the American Northwest and the history of the church in the United States. What is especially attractive is the way Rippinger weaves biographical sketches of interesting community members and in-depth treatment of various works of the Abbey into the overall historical narrative. The framework of 'struggle and ascent' enables him to treat head-on the missteps and scandals that occurred while finding good reason to affirm the resilience, the faith, and the contribution to the life of the church in the Pacific Northwest that rightly characterizes the monks of Mount Angel Abbey through the decades."

    —Abbot Benedict Neenan, OSB
        Conception Abbey, Conception Missouri

"As a protestant pastor and Benedictine oblate with Mount Angel, I've made regular pilgrim retreats every year up to Mount Angel Abbey over the past two decades. The vision from the hilltop reminds me of being at Monte Cassino, where Benedict wrote in the Rule that we ascend by descending along steps of humility. Following the steps and pages of this well-written historic narrative, through the many challenges and celebrations of life in community, we see anew the vision of Benedict's Rule lived out daily among the monks through lives of stability, fidelity, and obedience to Christ since the 1880s."

    —Rev. Dr. David Robinson
        Oblate of Mount Angel Abbey, author of *Cloud Devotion: Through the Year with The Cloud of Unknowing*, and Lead Pastor, Cannon Beach Community Church, Cannon Beach, Oregon

"In the footsteps of their monastic predecessors, Benedictines arrived in the Willamette Valley in 1882 to build up the church and culture through their prayer and work. Fr. Joel's narrative of Mount Angel Abbey vividly portrays the cross at the center of monastic life, manifesting its power through human weakness. Mount Angel, persevering through the flaws of its leaders and a multitude of calamities, such as fire, presents an image of the entire church, stably standing on the mountaintop through all difficulties."

    —R. Jared Staudt, PhD
        Archdiocese of Denver and Augustine Institute, author of *The Beer Option*

Struggle and Ascent

The History of Mount Angel Abbey

Joel Rippinger, OSB

Foreword by
Abbot Jeremy Driscoll, OSB

LITURGICAL PRESS
Collegeville, Minnesota

www.litpress.org

Cover design by Tara Wiese. Cover and interior photographs courtesy of Mount Angel Abbey Archives.

1	2	3	4	5	6	7	8	9

Library of Congress Cataloging-in-Publication Data

Names: Rippinger, Joel, 1948– author.
Title: Struggle and ascent : the history of Mount Angel Abbey / Joel Rippinger, OSB.
Description: Collegeville, Minnesota : Liturgical Press, 2020. | Summary: "The history of Mount Angel Abbey as the history of a pilgrim Church, a steady and transformative sign of God's kingdom on earth"— Provided by publisher.
Identifiers: LCCN 2019055208 (print) | LCCN 2019055209 (ebook) | ISBN 9780814665039 (paperback) | ISBN 9780814665275 (epub) | ISBN 9780814665275 (mobi) | ISBN 9780814665275 (pdf)
Subjects: LCSH: Mt. Angel Abbey (Saint Benedict, Or.)—History. | Abbeys—Oregon—Saint Benedict—History. | Benedictines—Oregon— Saint Benedict—History. | Monastic and religious life—Oregon—Saint Benedict—History. | Saint Benedict (Or.)—Church history.
Classification: LCC BX2525.S225 R56 2020 (print) | LCC BX2525.S225 (ebook) | DDC 271/.1079537—dc23
LC record available at https://lccn.loc.gov/2019055208
LC ebook record available at https://lccn.loc.gov/2019055209

To my parents, Joseph and Helen Rippinger,
whose model of service and stability sustained my
Benedictine vocation and who both went to the Lord
as I was writing this history

Contents

Foreword

*S*TRUGGLE AND ASCENT—this brief title summarizes the history of Mount Angel Abbey, a Benedictine monastery in the state of Oregon, of which I am the twelfth abbot. As of this writing, our monastery has existed for 138 years, and the story of those years is a gripping one. Certainly there is *struggle*, both to establish a monastery and then to survive. And the monastic charism itself is also about a spiritual struggle. With the struggle there is also *ascent*—on a literal level the establishing of the monastery on a hilltop in the middle of the Willamette Valley, and on a spiritual level, the fruits of the struggle. These are archetypal patterns of the monastic life, the striving and desiring that characterize it, the combination of horizontal and vertical movements both at once.

It is with joy and satisfaction that I introduce this volume of Fr. Joel Rippinger's history of Mount Angel Abbey. I myself have lived here as a monk for the last fifty years. Orally, I know many of the stories of our history, and fifty years is some of the story, too. I knew for many reasons that it would be good to have a careful account of this history, a setting down of events and consequences in an order that they could be shared and understood. I hoped for a serious reflection on the significance of all that has happened at Mount Angel in decade after decade of faithful, though never easy, monastic living.

So, shortly after I became abbot in 2016, I approached Fr. Joel and invited him to research and write our history. I knew that he was someone who could do this and that he had already done a good deal of the remote preparation needed for such a project. I knew this from his valuable history of *The Benedictine Order in the United States, an Interpretive History.* In that book, Mount Angel's history was briefly fitted into the history of the whole Benedictine movement in this country, beginning in the middle of the nineteenth century and continuing into the present. I remember reading that book years ago and sensing then that its author would have much more he could say about Mount Angel if given the opportunity. Now I was in a position to offer him that opportunity. With the gracious consent of his religious superior, Abbot John Brahill of Marmion Abbey, Fr. Joel enthusiastically accepted my invitation to research and write a history of Mount Angel Abbey.

We agreed that I would give him complete access to our archives and leave him entirely free in his interpretation and presentation of the story. It was to be a story told from the outside, with the objective standards of a trained historian and the familiarity that a monk himself would have with the nature of the monastic materials he was handling. The results are here, and it is these results that give me the joy and satisfaction I already mentioned in being able to present this volume.

I confess that one of my interests in having this history written has to do with my own monastery and its monks in the present times. Younger monks especially, but even monks of my generation and older, do not really know the details of how much hardship, setback, and resilience have made it possible for us to live the monastic life we have here today. A remarkable heritage and tradition have been bequeathed to us by those who preceded us here. It would be unseemly, to say the least, to live our lives today unaware of the deep values and sacrifices that have made Mount Angel what it is today.

Every monastery has a unique face, style, atmosphere, mood, and energy. This comes from the vow of stability that Benedictines make, a vow that binds them to a place and to a particular community for life. And in each place a monastery must make changes as it moves forward in new times, facing new situations that emerge often only in that particular place and with that particular group of monks. It is a monastic ethos to cling close to origins, to receive from one's elders an already well-established way, to carry on with what has been received even while facing new situations and so changing accordingly. As abbot, wanting to instill in my own community this ethos, I saw that this history could help me. I want us at Mount Angel to be able to say, yes, there is a monastic way of doing things and within that way, there is also a Mount Angel way. Father Joel's history is the story of the shaping of that Mount Angel way. How did it come about that we at Mount Angel are who we are today? And given that, how do we regard this treasure received, and when do we risk change? I am asking the question that stands behind the motto of my predecessor Abbot Bonaventure: *Nova et Vetera*, new things and old. Indeed, new things and old. "What will it be?" is the question every monastery faces every day in all its monastic ways and practices.

What I just explained is a more personal reason for wanting this history. I also wanted it to be known to a larger public because I know that the story could deservedly draw the attention of anyone interested in the history of monasticism in this country and, indeed, in church history in general in the United States and beyond. This is a story that edifies but can also raise eyebrows and even, occasionally, shock. There is deep holiness and fortitude, but also broken vows and ill-advised decisions. There is fire that destroys, and more than once; and there is embezzlement and abuse and sometimes almost no money to go forward. And yet the place and the enterprise survive and even in some seasons thrive.

Is this not the mystery of the whole church? Are there not lessons here also for other monasteries and other parts of the church and also for those who just observe religious quest in general or the human drama in general? What happens when people search for God, when they try hard to build something, when they try to give themselves completely away? Mount Angel's history demonstrates in many concrete ways what the monastic virtues are, what the monastic contribution is to church and world, what are the struggles of many and most of us in trying to persevere in a task for a lifetime. Sharing Mount Angel's story with a wider audience is another reason I wanted Fr. Joel to write this history. Mount Angel's story told is not boasting. There is nothing to boast about here. This story is a celebration of grace—of God's faithfulness to us, of God's mercy and forgiveness, of the fruits of trusting in God. Grace's story shows as well how much God can bring out of persons in trials, struggles, and darkness. We are still here. A miracle, a huge grace. The story of the whole church. The story of Mount Angel.

Still another reason prompted me to invite Fr. Joel to the task he has so ably performed with this history. The year 2020 is the 900th anniversary of the founding in 1120 of our monastic motherhouse, Engelberg, in Switzerland. It has had a continuous existence since then. Fr. Joel's story of Mount Angel situates its founding by Engelberg in the context of events in Switzerland in the mid-nineteenth century. Those events led to the founding by Engelberg of, first, another monastery in the United States, Conception Abbey, in Missouri. For the complex reasons that are told in the history recounted here, some Engelberg monks from that Conception foundation split from the original group of its founding party of monks and eventually established Mount Angel. But that inception of Mount Angel was fragile in the extreme. Mount Angel would never have survived without the commitment and, alas, the suffering and worry of the heroic and wise abbot of Engelberg, Anselm Villiger. But not only that. Without Abbot Frowin Conrad of Conception—originally a monk of Engelberg and from whom Mount Angel's party of founders had separated themselves—Mount Angel would never have survived. Father Joel recounts here the role of Abbot Anselm and Abbot Frowin, and he relates a story heretofore untold, throwing into clear relief what crucial players they were in carrying Mount Angel through its turbulent and fragile first decades.

Adelhelm Odermatt, Mount Angel's founder, was also a gifted monk that Engelberg sacrificed to its adventure in America. He was both the inspiration of so much of Mount Angel's unique monastic face and also, somehow not infrequently, the source of some of its most serious early problems. Abbot Anselm of Engelberg guided him, corrected him, chided him, and encouraged him, expressing in all this a fondness and love for the Mount Angel project. He urged Abbot Frowin to do the same and gave him special authority to do so in a monastery that was still canonically dependent upon Engelberg. Father Adelhelm accepted all this—usually with humility—and carried on. Meanwhile, other monks from Engelberg, some of their best from that epoch, were sent by Abbot Anselm to Mount Angel. Some came for a while; others ended their long lives at Mount Angel. In short, during those nine hundred years of Engelberg's continuous monastic life, some decades of the last half of the nineteenth century and the first decades of the twentieth were years in which that venerable monastery sacrificed much to pour its spirit into two American houses: Conception and Mount Angel. That spirit still lives in all three monastic houses, unique in each place but also clearly one same family. So, this history means also to be a tribute to Engelberg in its 900th year and a profound thank you from the depths of Mount Angel's heart to its beloved motherhouse.

Finally, both Fr. Joel and I feel the privilege of publishing this monastic history with Liturgical Press of St. John's Abbey. This press through its long existence has contributed so much to the making known of monastic history and theology and even more to what all monks hold dear—namely, the liturgy itself, its history, and its deepest significance. To have Mount Angel's history included among the projects of Liturgical Press is an honor not lost on us. I sincerely hope this story told can be a celebration for all the Benedictine monasteries of this country. We are planted in this land from such solid origins in Europe, of which our holy father St. Benedict is the patron.

As he would say: *Ut in omnibus glorificetur Deus!*

Abbot Jeremy Driscoll, OSB
Abbot of Mount Angel Abbey

Preface

MONASTERIES ARE THE REPOSITORIES of stories. Mount Angel Abbey has witnessed a generous catalogue of those stories in its faith-filled passage from the nineteenth to the twenty-first century. The intent of this historical narrative is to introduce readers to the larger story of Mount Angel. It is one interpretation of that story, given through the lens of someone who comes from outside the Mount Angel monastic community. However, it comes from the perspective of an observer who carries a deep appreciation for this story and the characters who shaped it. For many years I have worked with historical material that has allowed me to become familiar with some of the major figures in the Mount Angel history. I also have benefited from studying it within the wider narrative of American Benedictine history. In the process, it has become evident to me that this is a story that deserves to be told and to have a wider audience.

Like so many other monasteries, Mount Angel has had its share of challenges. Its two great fires and the community's subsequent determination to rebuild are markers of the resolve displayed by monks in the face of adversity. The anti-Catholicism and anti-German prejudice they experienced were of a piece with what many of their fellow monasteries suffered, though there was a distinct quality to the way those prejudices played out in the state of Oregon. Mount Angel, like most monasteries, had its cast of colorful characters. This roster of characters includes outstanding leaders and men of great holiness. The educational legacy left by Mount Angel is one that loomed large in the historical record of the Northwest. That legacy of teaching broadened beyond Oregon to embrace Native American outposts in remote islands, foundations in Canada and Mexico, and the personal witness of monks who became known as master teachers and scholars.

The history of any monastic community is closely aligned with the unique features of its place and the people it serves. This is partly due to the charism of Benedictine stability. It is also due to a factor that can never be overlooked in the course of monastic history—the indelible imprint left on a place and people by a community of vowed members, a monastic cohort committed to giving a witness to the Gospel and to a venerable standard of holiness as realized in the Benedictine tradition of a love of learning and a desire for God.

There was, from the earliest years, a clear and compelling witness from monks at Engelberg Abbey in Switzerland and Conception Abbey in Missouri that the mission of the monastic founders of Mount Angel was one that was worthy of their support. This became evident even in the most precarious and trying stretches of Mount Angel's history. No amount of financial insecurity or scandal or setback could stay the force of that faith. Left to its own resources and human potential, one can only question Mount Angel's ability to survive through the early years of its history. It received help from a medley of sources that helped to lift the fortunes of the community in its pioneer period.

It is my sincere hope that the history of Mount Angel Abbey will serve as a stimulus for a wider audience to draw from the lessons and learn from the human models that were so instrumental in that history. My personal wish is that the faith that carried the Mount Angel community through many physical challenges and moral crises will serve as an animating force in promoting a greater understanding of the monastic tradition for the benefit of future generations.

Acknowledgments

THE WRITING OF THE HISTORY of Mount Angel Abbey is an undertaking that merits acknowledgment of a variety of people and sources.

I will start with Abbot Jeremy Driscoll of Mount Angel. It was Abbot Jeremy who first invited me to take on this task, granting assurance of his personal support and the resources of his community. Among those personal resources is Fr. Augustine DeNoble, longtime archivist of the Abbey, whose familiarity with the written sources of Mount Angel's history and whose personal recollections of the same were invaluable aids. Br. Cyril Drnjevic and Br. Ansgar Santogrossi were most helpful assistants in the project, contributing their time and expertise in research and wise counsel on procuring material for the history. Archivist Brian Morin and his staff in the community archives, particularly Elizabeth Uhlig, proved to be ready and willing resources in scanning photos and retrieving added information from the rich trove of the abbey's archival holdings. Among the personal interviews I conducted with the monks of the community, special thanks go to former abbots Peter Eberle, Nathan Zodrow, and Gregory Duerr and to the current abbot, Jeremy Driscoll. The hospitality afforded me by the Mount Angel community over several years has been another gift that is part of this project. Having a place of prayer and beauty in which to do research was a beneficial by-product of my work.

I need to give thanks to my own superior of Marmion Abbey, Abbot John Brahill, for providing permission to undertake this project and allowing me the time and space needed to complete it. All of my confreres at Marmion Abbey deserve to be included in that, especially as they have given me the latitude to finish the project.

Liturgical Press deserves a note of gratitude as well. Their willingness to provide their professional assistance in editing and publishing this book is deeply appreciated. Peter Dwyer and Hans Christoffersen were wise and supportive publishers, and Stephanie Lancour was a patient and extremely helpful production editor.

Lastly, I owe a sincere gratitude to several generations of monks of Mount Angel Abbey, whose faith and determination to give an authentic Benedictine witness provided me with the means to narrate a story with elements of heroism, holiness, and hardship. It is a story that attests to the richness of the historical legacy of Benedictine life in Europe and America, and the countless graces that continue to flow from such a vibrant life lived in seeking God. My sincere hope is that in sharing this story the invaluable gift of monastic life and those who support it will be duly enriched.

CHAPTER ONE

European Background

L IKE SO MUCH OF AMERICAN HISTORY, the record of American Benedictines is closely tied to the European continent. For the monks of Mount Angel, the connection rests with the Abbey of Engelberg in Switzerland. The stimulus that led to German-speaking Swiss monks coming to Oregon in the 1880s is part of a complex chain of events. Examining those events and the people at their center constitutes an essential beginning to Mount Angel's history. There remains at the heart of Mount Angel's effort to develop a distinct monastic identity a spiritually genetic strand of firmness of purpose and sense of duty that hearkens back to the Swiss motherhouse.

The Swiss Abbey of Engelberg dates back to the twelfth century. Much like its American foundation in Oregon, it suffered loss through a succession of destructive fires, as well as the ravages resulting from the Protestant Reformation, the Enlightenment, and the Napoleonic Wars. The monastic membership of the community came close to extinction with an outbreak of the plague in the late sixteenth century. The most damaging of the fires in the first half of the eighteenth century totally destroyed the abbey church and required extensive rebuilding. Much of the struggle between political authority and religious autonomy that precipitated a crisis for Engelberg in the nineteenth century was focused in the *Sonderbund*, the Swiss civil war that began in 1847. In the wake of that conflict, a number of Benedictine educational institutions in the country were secularized, and some monastic communities were suppressed.

Painting depicting Engelberg Abbey and its surrounding valley in central Switzerland.

Abbot Anselm Villiger, the fifty-second abbot of Engelberg Abbey and founder of Mount Angel Abbey.

Because of the fear of possible suppression, the Swiss Abbey of Einsiedeln sent monks to North America in 1854, where they established a community in Saint Meinrad, Indiana. Among the motives for this move was that of securing a possible American refuge for Einsiedeln Abbey in case of closure by the Swiss civil authorities.

It was in these tumultuous years that Engelberg Abbey elected a new abbot, Anselm Villiger. He became abbot in 1866 and continued in that role until his death in 1901, a remarkable span of thirty-five years. He was to play an integral role in the establishment and growth of Mount Angel. The clos-

Fr. Frowin Conrad (left) and
Fr. Adelhelm Odermatt (right)
at Engelberg, prior to their
departure to North America
in 1873.

est observers of the beginning stages of Mount Angel's development
rightly credit the determination and guidance of Abbot Anselm as
perhaps the most telling factor in Mount Angel's spiritual and material viability.

There were two other figures in the community at Engelberg who
were central to the early history of Mount Angel. One was Fr. Frowin
Conrad. Father Frowin, the eldest of twelve children, made his monastic profession at Engelberg in 1853 and was ordained to the priesthood in 1858. In the first fifteen years of his priesthood at Engelberg,
he served as a prefect and professor in the school, pastor at the local
parish, novice master, librarian, and chaplain to the Benedictine Sisters in nearby Maria Rickenbach. He also spent time in theological
studies at the Abbey of Einsiedeln, where he made the acquaintance
of Fr. Martin Marty, a young priest-monk of the Abbey of Einsiedeln
who was to become the principal founder of Einsiedeln's first American
foundation of St. Meinrad in Indiana, and a prominent figure in persuading Engelberg to make its initial American foundation.

The other member of the Engelberg community who served as a central figure in Mount Angel's founding and early history was Fr. Adelhem Odermatt. Entering Engelberg in 1865, he had Fr. Frowin as his novice master. He was then an assistant to Fr. Frowin in the parish of Engelberg and a professor at Engelberg's school. Father Frowin's junior by eleven years, Fr. Adelhem was a visible contrast to him both in personality and physical bearing. The bearded and solidly built younger monk towered over the diminutive and clean-shaven Fr. Frowin. One of the more graphic descriptions of Fr. Adelhelm was given by Fr. Edward Malone, the historian of Conception Abbey, who highlights some of his distinctive personality traits: "Father Adelhelm . . . manages to give the impression of a mild ecclesiastical boomer, but at the same time the deep dedication and inexhaustible energy of the dedicated missionary are clearly discernible. He is the always enthusiastic Swiss and the nostalgic Engelberger."[1] Anyone who traces the stages of Fr. Adelhelm's monastic life cannot help but detect in his person a continuous current of religious zeal, one that was accompanied by an outspoken and sanguine temperament. He was the yang to Fr. Frowin's quiet and reflective monastic yin.

Beginnings in North America

It was the former classmate of Fr. Frowin, Abbot Martin Marty, who became the precipitator of Engelberg's initial venture in North America. In 1872, Abbot Martin, as the recently elected first abbot of St. Meinrad Abbey, referred a request from Bishop John Hogan of Saint Joseph, Missouri, to have a Benedictine presence in his diocese to the Abbey of Engelberg. At the same time, Abbot Martin sent several letters to his friend Fr. Frowin, urging him to have his community accept the request, knowing that the Engelberg community was facing the same fear of dissolution that Einsiedeln had faced years earlier. One can presume that the letter had its desired effect, since the Engelberg chapter of monks voted in January of 1873 to accept the request from Bishop Hogan in Missouri.

1. Edward Malone, OSB, *Conception* (Omaha, NE: Interstate Printing, 1971), 119.

The expectation of Engelberg Abbey for the proposed new foundation might best be calculated on what they had witnessed in other monastic foundations made in the United States in previous decades. The string of monasteries founded by Abbot Boniface Wimmer, from his first Benedictine community in Latrobe, Pennsylvania, in 1846, was marked by an activist thrust of service to immigrant Catholic populations that were largely, but not exclusively, German-speaking. They included an educational component of schools for immigrants and seminaries that would serve to staff the sacramental needs of the local churches. Lay brothers constituted a large part of the composition of these communities, and the monks worked in concert with communities of Benedictine women that had been established nearby. The foundation made by Einsiedeln Abbey at St. Meinrad, Indiana, in 1854, mirrored some of these same characteristics. Extensive parish work was accepted at St. Meinrad as both a service to the immigrant and a means of material support for the community. A seminary school was started and a nearby community of Benedictine sisters was established. Whether consciously or not, Engelberg would employ many of these same elements in the monasteries they established in America, along with their purported wish to have a geographic refuge from the potential perils of European politics.

Missouri Roots

So it was that Fathers Frowin and Adelhelm left Engelberg for the United States in early 1873. On the way, Fr. Frowin stopped at the Abbey of Beuron in Germany. There he was to meet with the two founders of that monastery, Abbot Maurus Wolter and his brother Fr. Placidus Wolter. Father Frowin was given from the abbot a *Ceremoniale*, a liturgical book of ceremonies, that he intended to use as needed upon arrival in America. When the two Engelberg pioneer monks arrived in New York in May, they made their way across the eastern United States, stopping in Pennsylvania, where they met with Abbot Boniface Wimmer at St. Vincent's Abbey in Latrobe. They then traveled to St. Meinrad, Indiana, where they were welcomed by Fr. Frowin's friend, Abbot Martin Marty. Fathers Frowin and Adelhelm were invited to spend several months at St. Meinrad, honing their language skills and

A postcard image of Conception Abbey from the early 1900s.

also deriving benefit from Abbot Martin's advice on how to go about making a new monastic foundation in America. Father Fintan Mundwiler, Abbot Martin's prior at St. Meinrad, did the necessary advance work in Missouri with Bishop Hogan to prepare adequate lodgings on site for the Engelberg monks. In September of 1873, Fr. Frowin and Fr. Adelhelm traveled to Conception, Missouri, to begin their work.

Father Frowin was aware of the desire of Abbot Anselm Villiger to secure a place of refuge in the United States as a result of the threats by the Swiss government to close Catholic institutions. The Engelberg community made this clear in the chapter minutes of that year when they declared that, in the event of the suppression of Engelberg, the American foundation was to give asylum to any members of the Engelberg community.[2] At the same time, Fr. Frowin was intent upon establishing a truly monastic community, rooted in the best traditions of Benedictine prayer and observance. By contrast, Fr. Adelhelm's main intent was on developing a pastoral presence among the immigrant Catholics of Nodaway County, Missouri. Within the first few years,

2. Copies of chapter minutes of July 20, 1873, from Engelberg, translated copy in Mount Angel Abbey Archives (hereafter MAAA).

their differing ideals of Benedictine life became more obvious. Father Frowin served as superior of the monastic community at Conception and employed the liturgical and monastic practices of the German Abbey of Beuron to lay the basis of what he hoped would be a solidly formed Benedictine monastery. Father Adelhelm lived apart in the nearby town of Maryville, where he exercised a role as both parish priest and superior over a house of monks and of Benedictine sisters who had come from Switzerland. The separate monastic paths the two Swiss founders adopted were becoming more defined.

By 1875 tensions began to appear between the more cloistered ideal of monastic life advocated by Fr. Frowin and a more actively engaged one of Fr. Adelhelm. These differing points of view were channeled through letters that Fr. Adelhelm sent back to Engelberg and Abbot Anselm. The flashpoint of those tensions was what Fr. Adelhelm characterized as an overly partial emphasis Fr. Frowin was giving at Conception to the practices and model of the German Abbey of Beuron rather than to the Swiss customs of the motherhouse. There was substance to Fr. Adelhelm's critique. By this time, Fr. Frowin had been in frequent contact with Fr. Placidus Wolter of Beuron. He had adapted the *Ceremoniale* at Conception and was intending to possibly send young monks at Conception to Beuron for part of their formation. Father Adelhelm's critical opinions on what he saw at Conception were reinforced by those of a monk of Einsiedeln, Fr. Ignatius Conrad, a brother of Fr. Frowin, who had taken up residence in Maryville. Reactions to these letters appear in the diary of Abbot Anselm in 1875 and 1876 and they were sharply critical of the Conception superior.[3] The ensuing rebuke that Fr. Frowin received from Abbot Anselm in an 1876 letter, with its implied threat to replace Fr. Frowin with Fr. Adelhelm as superior at Conception if the Beuronese practices were not discontinued, was a bitter blow for Fr. Frowin. But he was obedient to the Engelberg abbot's command, and he tried for a time to implement Swiss customs at Conception in place of those of Beuron. What was

---

3. The diary of Anselm Villiger is an invaluable tool for understanding Abbot Anselm's views on the foundations in North America. A monk of Mount Angel, Fr. Ambrose Zenner, translated substantial sections of that diary while working at Engelberg. It is those translations, found in MAAA, that are used here.

now clear to Fr. Frowin was that Fr. Adelhelm and his own brother Fr. Ignatius were the principal players in convincing Abbot Anselm of the "harm" being done through the Beuronese practices.

Father Frowin rededicated himself to nurturing a monastic community at Conception, an effort that would result in achieving independence from Engelberg in 1881, when he was appointed as the first abbot of Conception. This appointment reflected on the part of Engelberg a less rigid insistence on the American house following to the letter all of the customs of its Swiss motherhouse than had previously been the case.

During this time, Fr. Adelhelm continued to reside at Maryville. There he cultivated an alternate monastic model, staying at arm's length from Conception's community. In the course of his seven years there, he incurred a substantial debt, much to the chagrin of Fr. Frowin. It was to be a harbinger of things to come. Unlike most of the other monks in Missouri, Fr. Adelhelm expressed his reluctance to transfer his vow of stability from Engelberg to Conception. In fact, he had already promoted the independence of a group of Benedictine sisters allied with him in Maryville, and this seemed to spark an interest in his doing the same for monks. For a time, Fr. Adelhelm considered making a separate monastic foundation in Maryville. Not providing Fr. Frowin with any information on this plan only sowed more seeds of suspicion on the part of Fr. Frowin once he found this out.

With a mixture of hurt and surprise, Fr. Frowin wrote in his journal:

> Today I received through Father Ignatius [Conrad] a copy of the letter our Rt. Rev. Abbot has written to the Bishop [Hogan] of St. Joseph, to recommend to him the Fathers Nicholas and Adelhelm for support in founding a new monastery here [in Missouri]. It is dated January 6. The contents of this letter appear to me unexplainable in many regards. May the Lord turn this whole trial to our good.[4]

Nor did it sit well with Bishop Hogan, who believed one monastery in his diocese was quite enough. Bishop Hogan too was wary of the im-

---

4. Journal of Frowin Conrad, February 11, 1881. Fr. Frowin's *Tagebuch*, or journal, remains a prized primary document. It records the key events in Mount Angel's history over the course of almost fifty years. A partially translated copy exists in the Archives of Conception Abbey (hereafter CAA).

pulsive character of Fr. Adelhelm's plans and did not contemplate kindly what he considered a maverick plan to build a replica of a Swiss Abbey in his diocese.

All the while Fr. Adelhelm continued his written correspondence with Abbot Anselm, presenting to him a plan that would permit him to make another monastic foundation, separate from Conception Abbey. By the close of 1880, Fr. Frowin was resigned to the fact that Fr. Adelhelm would not become a member of Conception Abbey and was intent upon starting his own new Benedictine community. In that same time, Fr. Adelhelm won over a fellow monk of Engelberg, Fr. Nicholas Frei, to assist him in carrying out his pioneering project. The disappointment all of this engendered on the part of Fr. Frowin is registered in an entry in his journal in early 1881:

Fr. Nicholas Frei, a monk of Engelberg, accompanied Fr. Adelhelm on his search for a site for Mount Angel.

> Father Adelhelm has allowed his worldly spirit to grow and he no longer even wears the cowl. This division among us has not left a good impression on the bishop. The whole affair has caused me great grief and it all came without my knowledge. I do not believe that if the bishop were in the possession of all the facts he would so easily have given permission for this private enterprise. But unfortunately, a decision has been reached without giving me the time to make my views known. My talks with Father Nicholas [Frei] have convinced me that our views of religious life are so far apart that we could never agree. Father Adelhelm, it seems to me, paints too rosy a picture of the prospects for a new foundation.[5]

5. Journal translation of Frowin Conrad, February 17, 1881, CAA.

Father Frowin's apprehension and intuition about the projected monastery proved to be well founded. It did not help that Fr. Adelhelm's departure left him with the need to replace a well-loved pastor at Maryville and the likelihood of Engelberg Abbey focusing its material and personal resources not on Conception, but on its *Neue Engelberg*.

Looking for a New Engelberg

Fathers Adelhelm and Nicholas departed from Maryville at the end of May in 1881. They had received permission from Abbot Anselm to explore areas of America's West to find a locale for a new community. At this point in Engelberg's history, the option for an American refuge was still very much in play. Abbot Anselm indicated as much in a letter sent in early January of 1881:

> From the beginning of this priory, the ordo, customs and traditions of the motherhouse at Engelberg will be carried out in as praiseworthy a manner as possible, and observed exactly, so that my confreres may find for themselves in America an acceptable and friendly refuge . . . should our monastery and common life be dissolved by the wicked government of Switzerland.[6]

Father Adelhelm, in particular, entertained a conviction that the West would offer the best choice of options for the new monastery. A template for him was the expansion of the monasteries of Abbot Boniface Wimmer and the American Cassinese Congregation whose spread had grown westward.[7] Father Ambrose Zenner, after intensive study of the correspondence between Fr. Adelhelm and Engelberg, attributed to the former the notion of building up a string of monastic houses along the West Coast of the United States, all of them dependent upon a Swiss motherhouse. The communities would be sustained by farming and parish work, and they would concentrate on spreading the faith to the local populace. The plan was significant not only for its grandiosity

6. Letter of Anselm Villiger, January 6, 1881, translated copy in MAAA.

7. Letter of Adelhelm Odermatt to Anselm Villiger, October 19, 1881, translation in MAAA. In this letter Odermatt envisioned the states of California, Oregon, and the territory of Washington, all offering the promise of locations for future monasteries.

of scale but for its understandable dependency on a European source for initial personnel and funding. It was a plan that never received any formal approval on the part of the monastic chapter at Engelberg, but one that propelled the early exploration of Fr. Adelhelm.

The travels of Fr. Adelhelm and Fr. Nicholas took them to Nebraska, the Dakota Territory (where they encountered then Bishop Martin Marty and Abbot Fintan Mundwiler of St. Meinrad), Colorado, Utah, Nevada, and California, as well as Oregon and the Washington Territory. They had the opportunity to spend time first in Denver with Bishop Machbeuf, in Pueblo, in largely Mormon Salt Lake City, in the area of Archbishop Joseph Alemany's San Francisco archdiocese and Bishop Francis Mora's Los Angeles diocese. The two monks left San Francisco on July 26 by boat and arrived in Portland on August 3, where they met Archbishop Charles Seghers. In the following weeks, they visited the Rogue River country near Jacksonville and the Willamette Valley near the towns of Fillmore and Sublimity.

In the time since their departure from Missouri, the two Swiss monks managed to traverse much of the western landscape of the United States. As they considered all of their options, it only whetted their appetite for the unbounded potential of a new Benedictine monastery that would be planted in that landscape.

The view that Fr. Nicholas carried of America after his western journey was not at great variance from that of his fellow traveler. It employed a mixture of pessimism about the prospects of monasticism's future in Switzerland and optimism about the potential of America. Writing to Abbot Anselm from Oregon, Fr. Nicholas echoed these two contrasting sentiments:

> I want to look at things as calmly as possible. Yet I can't help but think that Engelberg needs to take advantage of the present opportunity offered to it. Assuming the worst, the Swiss monasteries and other houses are likely to be swept away. If that is the case, I could not see any more pleasant and suitable locale for our confreres than this valley. What a huge area of activity is given to American monasteries is something with which you are already familiar.[8]

---

8. Letter of Nicholas Frei to Abbot Anselm Villiger, August 15, 1881, archives of Engelberg Abbey, translated copy in MAAA.

Both Fr. Adelhelm and Fr. Nicholas, after their meeting with a number of bishops on the West Coast, felt compelled to give serious consideration to the variety of sites they had explored in California and Oregon in 1881. During the whole of this time, Fr. Adelhelm was writing Abbot Anselm, giving him upbeat reports on the different possibilities. In California they had investigated the area in the northern part of the state with the appealing offer of free land in the area around Santa Inez, east of San Francisco. They had been given another attractive offer near Santa Barbara in the southern part of the state. In Oregon and the Washington Territory, their offers ranged from Walla Walla and Puget Sound in the Washington Territory to a medley of sites west of the Cascades in Oregon. They eventually narrowed down the "finalists" in their decision to a mission in northern California (Santa Inez in the Napa Valley), Jacksonville in the area of the Rogue River Valley in Oregon, and two spots in Oregon that were located in the upper Willamette Valley, south of Portland.

In the course of the selection process, the last place to have been visited in Oregon left the most favorable reactions. The two towns surrounding the Willamette Valley site, Fillmore and Sublimity, gave the monastic visitors both a gracious welcome and a promise of financial support when they arrived there in the fall of 1881. Father Adelhelm was further attracted to the Fillmore site because of the warm reception he received from the German-speaking Catholic families that had settled in the vicinity and the prospect of getting a number of non-German Protestant families to "donate" the land atop the hilltop to the visiting monks. Moreover, both Fillmore and Sublimity had access to a railroad, unlike the potential settlement in the Rogue River Valley. Father Adelhelm was given verbal assurance by the archbishop that the monastery would be given jurisdiction over the two German communities. All of this, and the similarities that Fr. Adelhelm made to the Oregon site and the Swiss countryside, seemed to be deciding factors in persuading him to give it preferential treatment. If Fr. Adelhelm needed more convincing, it came when he was taken to the butte outside of Fillmore known as *Tap-a-lam-a-ho*, or Mount of Communion, in the local Native American tribe dialect. Known also as Lone Butte Hill or Graves' Butte, atop the hill were stones said to provide arranged seats for prayer circles. The Native Americans, according to the local lore, would climb the hill to meditate on what they saw as sacred ground. It was the same site that Archbishop Seghers had visited shortly before the visit of the Benedictines, and both Fr. Adelhelm and the archbishop had similar reactions that this was a place for a monastery.[9]

It is noteworthy that Archbishop Seghers at the same time had invited Abbot Alexius Edelbrock of St. John's Abbey in Minnesota to come to Oregon with the invitation to assume pastoral care and educational efforts for the Native American missions. In response, Abbot Alexius made a visit to Oregon in December of 1881, after which he decided not to commit his community to the venture.[10] He did meet, at the be-

Archbishop Charles Seghers, the second archbishop of Oregon City, who invited Frs. Adelhelm Odermatt and Nicholas Frei to make a foundation in Oregon.

hest of Archbishop Seghers, with Fr. Adelhelm during his stay in the region. The reaction of both Benedictines can be characterized as surprise to know that they were "in competition" for making a monastic foundation.[11] Abbot Alexius then expressed an interest in a Northern California site on his West Coast trip. However, when he traveled to

9. Writing to Abbot Anselm, Fr. Adelhelm gave his glowing response to arriving at the present site of Mount Angel: "The view from the hill [in Fillmore] is magnificent. The archbishop and other competent people think that a monastery should be there." Letter of January 6, 1882, translated copy by Fr. Luke Eberle, MAAA.

10. John C. Scott, OSB, *The Place Called Saint Martin's 1895–1995* (Lacey, WA: Donning, 1996), 14–15. Several years later (1895), St. John's Abbey founded a community in the state of Washington at Lacey.

11. Lawrence McCrank, *Mt. Angel Abbey: A Centennial History of the Benedictine Community and Its Library, 1882–1982* (Wilmington, DE: Scholarly Resources, 1983), 28.

the same area of the Napa Valley that had been offered to the Engelberg monks and learned that Fr. Nicholas and Fr. Adelhelm had already engaged in discussion with Archbishop Alemany, he was rankled to have to "compete" with fellow Benedictines at both the California and Oregon sites, and he left for Minnesota without any immediate plans for bringing monks westward.

Father Nicholas spent time in California in the winter of 1881–82 for the professed intent of learning English and trying to pin down the invitation for the land offer and expectations made by the California bishops. It appeared that neither intent was achieved. Meanwhile, Fr. Adelhelm vigorously pursued pastoral duties at Gervais, Fillmore, and Sublimity, finding this triangle of small Oregon towns and their people to be a good fit for a future farm-based monastery that would be serving the needs of European immigrants with whom the monks could identify.

It was in March of 1882 that Fr. Adelhelm received word from Abbot Anselm to return to Engelberg, for the purpose of making a definitive decision on a location for the "New Engelberg" community. He left Oregon in early May, carrying a letter from Archbishop Seghers, giving the prelate's permission to make a request for the Engelberg monastic chapter to establish a Benedictine priory. The conditions in Switzerland had changed remarkably since the time of Fr. Adelhelm's departure for America in 1873. There was no longer an imminent threat of closure on the part of civil authorities. There was also awareness of changed conditions in North America—a thriving community of monks at Conception Abbey and a large contingent of Benedictine sisters from Maria Rickenbach who had split into two different communities at Conception and Maryville. There also seemed to be a number of members in the Engelberg community who were interested in volunteering for the American venture.

While Fr. Nicholas remained in Oregon, Fr. Adelhelm arrived at Engelberg in mid-June. He then presented the options of Oregon and California to Abbot Anselm, making his case for the Gervais/Sublimity and Fillmore site in Oregon. Abbot Anselm forwarded that recommendation to the Engelberg chapter. After some deliberation, it gave its approval in early July for the recommended Oregon foundation. The papal bull of permission was issued on July 16. Fathers Barnabas

Held, Bede Horat, and Anselm Wachter were all delegated by Abbot Anselm to accompany the troupe back to Oregon.[12] These were young monks who clearly would have made contributions to the Engelberg community had they remained and the sacrifice that the motherhouse was making was clearly in evidence.

Soon after that, Fr. Adelhelm began assembling an entourage that would accompany him back to Oregon. It included the already-mentioned three priest-monks and four choir monks from Engelberg, some would-be candidates (including the future Fr. Maurus Snyder), a mix of Benedictine sisters from the communities of Maria Rickenbach and Sarnen, and some Swiss lay workers. They were joined by a contingent of monks and novices who were going to Conception Abbey. There was no little consternation stirred within the Engelberg community by the hectic activity of gathering prayer books, habits, and monastic artifacts that would find their way into trunks and boxes that would accompany the sizeable group on their voyage across the ocean. By the time they were ready to leave Engelberg, the party had grown to about forty persons, about half of which were to go to Conception Abbey as monks or novices. Abbot Anselm in his diary expressed reservations about the speed at which Fr. Adelhelm cobbled together his equipment and secured his recruits. With respect to the latter, he was concerned over the lack of experience they had. He also had second thoughts about the considerable expense that would be incurred in the mission and the seemingly impulsive manner of accumulation of items that had become part of their train of travel. He wrote in his journal:

> What upsets me even more than the cost of the expedition is the fact that the people selected for this trip include too many who are lacking maturity in their vocation. On this very point I made my comments known and I now have little optimism about this expedition because in my opinion those who are leaving lack the necessary experience.[13]

The buoyant hopes Abbot Anselm had entertained for his New Engelberg just a year earlier now appeared to be tempered considerably. It was a posture that soon became even more pronounced as

12. McCrank, *Mt. Angel Abbey*, 31.
13. Journal translation of Anselm Villiger, September 8, 1882, MAAA.

the contingent left Switzerland and prepared to make decisions that would be further eroded by the difficulties in communication across the distance of an ocean and continent and by the frontier privations of western Oregon.

In the same month that the expedition was to leave Engelberg, September 1882, Abbot Frowin Conrad in Missouri expressed similar reservations about the new enterprise:

> It appears that there is a great enthusiasm in Engelberg for the foundation in Oregon, where a "pure" second Engelberg is proposed. I can only hope that my fears are not warranted. It seems to me that they have been overly impulsive in beginning the foundation and have not considered all of the difficulties that accompany a new beginning.[14]

Whatever reluctance may have been in place at the prospects of the pioneering contingent's likelihood of starting on firm footing, it carried from Switzerland the same inveterate optimism that marked the passage of pioneers who had gone to the Willamette Valley on the Oregon Trail from the interior of the United States a half century earlier. They readily identified as well with like-minded members of religious orders who at this same time with firmness of faith saw themselves as evangelizing agents for a frontier that was unbounded in its potential for spiritual fruit.

---

14. Translation of Journal of Frowin Conrad, September 22, 1882, CAA.

CHAPTER TWO

Beginnings of
the Oregon Foundation

The Arrival

THE NEWLY ORGANIZED EXPEDITION set out from Engelberg on September 25, 1882, being joined in Lucerne by Benedictine nuns from Sarnen. They arrived in New York City on October 11. They were met there by the Benziger Brothers, the reputable publishers of Catholic literature who had an office in New York and whose Swiss origins in Einsiedeln brought them dockside to meet the pilgrims on their way to the West Coast. The Swiss pilgrims were given a tour of the metropolis and thoughtfully provided with their cross-country rail itinerary. The train took them through the heartland and into northwest Missouri, where they parted with the members of their party who would stay on at Conception Abbey. There they also picked up a fellow Swiss, Sr. Bernadine Wachter, the sister of Fr. Anselm Wachter, who was to become the superior of the first Benedictine community of women in Mount Angel. Along with Sr. Bernadine, Sr. Johanna Zumstein, and several Benedictine sisters from the Sarnen community in Switzerland, they made the journey to the West Coast, seeking to establish a community.[1] Father Adelhelm left no written comment on this stopover

1. Mary Lucille Nachtsheim, OSB, *On the Way: The Journey of the Idaho Benedictine Sisters* (Cottonwood, ID: Twin Towers, 1997), 32–37. The Sarnen sisters settled first at the Grand Ronde Reservation in Oregon, then moved to Uniontown, Washington, and eventually to Idaho.

in Missouri, but there must have been a level of discomfort at work as his entourage of eager followers passed through Engelberg's first foundation in the United States and prepared to set out for what they considered to be the creation of a "New Engelberg." Some years later, Abbot Frowin, in a letter he sent to a monk of Engelberg, revealed how the pairing of Fr. Adelhelm and Fr. Nicholas did not evoke trust in the Conception superior:

> I cannot tell you how much it hurt me then and how abandoned I felt when Fr. Adelhelm and Fr. Nicholas set out with the blessing of Abbot Anselm to begin their own foundation. And even more the following year when they received the full approval and support of the chapter for their enterprise. I was almost certain they would fail and I made no secret of this to Abbot Anselm. . . . I knew both of the men too well—in spite of their striking abilities—to be able to put any faith in their beginning.[2]

They traveled by rail to San Francisco, where they were met by Archbishop Alemany (showing no ill feeling after the rejection of the Northern California offer), and then by steamer to Portland on October 28. While there, on October 30, they were met by a delegation of priests and officials from the local area. That latter date is recorded in the Swiss-American Congregation as the official foundation of the priory, and it is still observed today by the Mount Angel community as Founders' Day.

The contingent that constituted the first community of monks included a disparate grouping. There were five priests. In addition to Fr. Adelhelm and Fr. Nicholas, there were the three priests from Engelberg, Frs. Barnabas Held, Bede Horat, and Anselm Wachter, and one brother, Theodul Wursch. There were also seven frater novices (those who wished to study for the priesthood), along with two brother candidates.[3] They arrived at Gervais and settled there on October 31. Living quarters were to be in the parish house. The sisters who had come with Fr. Adelhelm were less fortunate. Accommodations were not yet ready for them, so they had to find temporary space in the former town

2. Letter of Abbot Frowin Conrad to Fr. Benedict Gottwald, 1896, translated copy, Archives of Conception Abbey (hereafter CAA).
3. Mount Angel Chapter Book, January 10, 1883, Mount Angel Abbey Archives (hereafter MAAA).

saloon, a disparity of primitive living conditions that was not unique to the Benedictine men and women of Oregon.[4]

Of Service to the Immigrant

The pioneer monks of Mount Angel were of a piece with their fellow Benedictines and many other Catholic religious orders from Europe that came to the United States in the nineteenth century. They felt an obligation to serve the sacramental and pastoral needs of the immigrant families whose numbers soared, especially in the last three decades of the century. For the German-speaking monks of Engelberg, a kinship was felt with the German-speaking farm families they met in the Willamette Valley. They identified with their agricultural life as well as their faith. They both realized they were part of a pioneer and pathfinding venture that would benefit by mutual assistance as they confronted the demands of a new country and culture.

Father Adelhelm felt a positive connection from the start with Matthias Butsch, at whose house he stayed on his original visit to Fillmore. It was Butsch who first took Fr. Adelhelm to the top of the butte that is the present site of Mount Angel. It was Butsch and his fellow farmers who wrote articles in German-American newspapers in support of European immigration to the Northwest. There was even an effort initiated by a German baron from Baden to buy up large tracts of land around Fillmore (soon to be renamed Mt. Angel) and have fifty-some immigrants from Germany and Switzerland come over to Oregon, settle on large tracts of relatively cheap land, and have a monastery with monks from Engelberg at its geographic and spiritual center.[5]

Three parishes had been entrusted to the administration of the monks by Archbishop Seghers at Gervais, Fillmore, and Sublimity. However, there was an urgent need to purchase land for the farming

4. See Alberta Dieker, OSB, "Rooted in Faith: The Early History of the Benedictine Sisters of Mt. Angel, Oregon," *American Benedictine Review* 58, no. 4 (December 2007), 362.

5. This elaborate plan that never saw reality is detailed at length in Lawrence McCrank, *Mt. Angel Abbey: A Centennial History of the Benedictine Community and Its Library, 1882–1982*, (Wilmington, DE: Scholarly Resources, 1983), 27–28.

The four buildings depicted are from left to right: St. Benedict Priory, Chapel, Seminary, and College. These buildings were destroyed in the 1892 fire.

needs of the community. That process took up much of the time and energy of Fr. Adelhelm in the next year. Purchase of the land required securing bank loans at high interest rates. It also required expenditures on the part of Engelberg far in excess of what they had expected. Abbot Anselm Villiger's diary entries in the latter part of 1883 register an increasing concern on his part over the financial weight being placed upon Engelberg, along with the difficulty of overseeing the land acquisitions of Fr. Adelhelm from such a distance. The land purchases were rendered more problematic because a large part of these tracts of land were the result of homesteads made by individual monks, acquisitions that were not certified until years later.[6] In the course of 1883, the economic plight of the Oregon priory steadily grew worse. Late frosts in the spring, forest fires, and a drought in the summer exacerbated the

6. Like a number of other monastic communities founded in the period after the Civil War, monks utilized the Homestead Act of 1862 to make individual claims on property of 160 acres that would accrue to the claimant—and the monastery—if the land were occupied and improved over the course of a five-year span.

growing debt of the fledgling community. Nonetheless, the numbers in the monastery continued to climb. By the close of 1883, there were twenty-five monks in the community. The first novice class consisted of five young men, one of whom was Maurus Snyder, who became the longest living member of the pioneer generation. Another young man who entered in 1883 was Medard Fuerst who, as Fr. Placidus, became the second abbot of Mount Angel. The fact that fifteen of the twenty-five monks were lay brothers is significant and quite in accord with other American Benedictine communities of that time.[7]

As a sign of confidence, the cornerstone for a new monastery at the Fillmore site was dedicated on May 11, 1884, and the Priory was officially transferred from Gervais to Mount Angel on July 14.[8] These signs of progress, however, could not mask the personal tensions that had emerged in the community. Father Nicholas felt estranged from Fr. Adelhelm after he had been replaced as procurator.[9] There was an increase in numbers of new recruits entering the community in these years, but the stability and formation they received were not always in evidence. Here, too, Abbot Anselm's reflections in his diary lament the inexperience and divisions within the community.[10]

By 1885 there was a new archbishop of Oregon City, William Gross. He had moved the seat of the archdiocese to Portland proper, even though the title was still in the name of Oregon City. More consequential for the priory, the new archbishop made a point of visiting the monastery in 1885. The archbishop was a member of the Redemptorist Order and showed a sensibility for the charism and history of the Benedictines. After his first visit to the community on August 1, the archbishop, showing insights derived from his own experience of living in a religious community, suggested that the monks curtail their

7. Statistics from a report submitted by Fr. Barnabas Held to Engelberg, December 8, 1883, CAA.

8. Records of foundation, MAAA. The name of Fillmore was changed to Mt. Angel in 1893, first for its post office and then as the "city of Mt. Angel."

9. After spending time in California and the Dakotas, Fr. Nicholas decided to return to Engelberg. His return trip across the Pacific in 1901 brought him to Calcutta, where he died on August 15, before reaching Switzerland.

10. Villiger, translation of journal entry for January 3, 1886, MAAA.

extensive parish work. His reasons for this counsel were contained in a letter he sent to Abbot Anselm that bears quoting:

> I consider it to be a very great mistake to allow the Fathers to look after parishes. Each Fr. who has such a parish is left to himself. He is not able to keep the Rule and is not under the supervision of a superior. . . . The great inclination toward freedom and independence in America is enough alone to penetrate a man's thinking, even though he is not in the midst of it, but when he is, he will lose without noticing it, all love for religious life and all interest in the choir and in school. He does not even wish to think about returning to monastic life with its choir obligation and other usages, and step by step he loses all the spirit of a Religious. For this reason I advise you, Fr. Abbot, in all politeness to send a command to Fr. Prior Adelhelm that he call all of the Fathers who are entrusted with parishes back to the monastery, and not allow the same in the future.[11]

The fact that Fr. Adelhelm had been immersed in parish work since his first arrival in Missouri made these words all the more trenchant. Archbishop Gross followed up on this urging by returning parishes at Gervais and Sublimity back to diocesan control. All of the above moves by the archbishop resulted in the decision by Fr. Adelhelm to open a seminary and college.

Whether it was in response to the archbishop's wish or not, the Benedictine community was incorporated under Oregon state law as an educational institution. The first school opened on October 22, 1887, and a considerable number of students (over 125) entered in the first year. The school's *Prospectus* included the objective "to impart to young men a thorough moral and mental training so as to fit them for any position in life."[12] Non-Catholics were allowed to enroll as long as they accepted the rigorous moral code and attended religious exercises. The school was very much in the German *gymnasium* tradition of a "classics" curriculum, with the notable exception of the option for students of engaging in agriculture as they worked in the fields with the monks.

---

11. Letter of Archbishop William Gross to Abbot Anselm Villiger, October 22, 1887, translation by Ambrose Zenner, quoted in Edward Malone, OSB, *Conception* (Omaha, NE: Interstate Printing, 1971), 225–26.

12. Prospectus of Mount Angel College (1887), MAAA.

This picture of Archbishop Gross with the community was taken during the retreat of 1888.

A seminary opened two years later in 1889, with Fr. Dominic Waedenschwyler, a recent arrival from Engelberg, as its first rector. It was the first seminary west of the Rocky Mountains to serve exclusively the new dioceses that were organized above California.[13] The enrollment in the seminary was sparse in early years, and so was any subsidy from the archdiocese. However, the seminary became a fixture in the mission of the monastery, and it grew in prestige over time. Archbishop Gross took an active interest in the college and seminary in subsequent years and the reputation that the schools acquired was a favorable one.

The Matter of the Land

Of all the initial decisions made by Fr. Adelhelm, the one to purchase large tracts of land in the area around Mount Angel would become among the most significant for the early course of the community's fortunes. After just over a decade of working in the United States, Fr. Adelhelm had learned the importance of acquiring land. He knew that a monastery required sufficient acreage for a farm operation, and that the initial construction of buildings for the monastery would be dependent on available options of land. He also had a memory from

13. Fr. Albert Bauman, "Fr. Dominic," *Mount Angel Letter* 34 (1982), 3–5.

his time at Engelberg of the practical priority of procuring forest and grazing land that would ensure the well-being of any monastery's economic stability.

One element in the western regions of the United States that became an even greater inducement for land acquisition in the second half of the nineteenth century was the 1862 Homestead Act. Under this legislation, any adult could occupy government land up to 160 acres and, if they could claim continual residence and improvement of the land over the course of five years, would be able to lay claim to it. This had been a key factor in the success of earlier Benedictine communities in the West such as St. John's Abbey in Minnesota, as individual monks lived on unclaimed tracts of land that were eventually acquired for the monastery. It seems that Fr. Adelhelm persuaded a number of the lay brothers of the community and some local settlers to homestead tracts of land surrounding the monastery. The classic case of this, inscribed in the early oral history of Mount Angel was the Stone House in the middle of Grassy Flats. The house was built at the intersection of four homesteads, and four separate persons took up residence at different rooms of the house, allowing for four different claims to be made on the surrounding land.[14]

More controversial was the decision of Fr. Adelhelm to make a number of purchases of land around the Fillmore site. He may have been encouraged by verbal promises made by a number of Catholic families in the area during his initial visit in 1881–82 to pledge money for land acquisitions. What became clear is that, from November of 1882 into the first months of 1883, Fr. Adelhelm made a series of land purchases that gave the community both the assurance of obtaining its most desired property of the butte and its surrounding land, and also a debt in the area of $74,000. All of these transactions were complicated by the fact that there was a lag time of some weeks in correspondence between Fr. Adelhelm and Abbot Anselm, and that Fr. Adelhelm was working with California investors through a Portland bank. Another difficulty was that the Abbey of Engelberg was putting up the money for the debt and coordinating through bankers in Lucerne with loans from

---

14. See Fr. William Hammelman, "The History of Mt. Angel Abbey's Mountain Land," *Mount Angel Letter* (October 1965), 3.

other monasteries in Switzerland.[15] Nor was it an easy task to translate American acreage into European units of measure and American dollars into Swiss francs. Yet Fr. Adelhelm remained resolute in his willingness to accept temporary debts. Writing to Abbot Anselm, he averred: "You have no idea of how repugnant this making of debts is to me, but all of us were always unanimous in doing so, convinced that it was high time to secure so much in order to make sure of the place and lay foundations for a happy future and to save the motherhouse eventually great expenditures."[16]

It remains unsure if the "all of us" in the correspondence was truly representative of all the members of the community, but no doubt Fr. Adelhelm believed it to be so. The most accurate accounts reflect that Mount Angel came close to going into liquidation or bankruptcy by the end of 1883. Although Fr. Adelhelm made some urgent pleas to local residents to pledge money, it was the Abbey of Engelberg that shouldered almost the full burden of the indebtedness. At a time when the very thought of bankruptcy for a religious institution was associated with shame and scandal, much angst was generated in the monasteries in Switzerland and America. Regardless of the long-term security the properties may have given to Mount Angel, it is undeniable that Fr. Adelhelm's vigorous pursuit of land acquisition and large loans in the first two years of Mount Angel's existence made for a tenuous financial condition and a less trusting regard for the new community's venture from the point of view of its Swiss motherhouse.

One saving initiative undertaken by Fr. Adelhelm was to both homestead and purchase substantial acreage of timberland in the hills surrounding Mount Angel. It was estimated that by 1886 the community had over 35,000 acres of timberland, most of it toward the western slopes of the Cascades.[17] The buying and selling of this timberland in the next century was to be a reliable source of income for the community when other means of drawing income were scarce.

15. McCrank, *Mt. Angel Abbey*, 37.

16. Letter of Odermatt to Anselm Villiger, August 13, 1883, translation in MAAA.

17. McCrank, *Mt. Angel Abbey*, 37. About 2,000 acres of timberland was homesteaded, and 1,360 acres were purchased from the Oregon and California Railroad.

The monastic community is pictured at the foot of the hill next to
the priory and college, May 1891.

While income was being derived from the remaining parishes that
the new community took on, it appeared evident that the monks of
Mount Angel needed to parlay their land investment with some pro-
ductive farming enterprise, as well as a building program that would
not overtax its limited means if the community were to reclaim fiscal
respectability.

Engelberg's Role

The bills that began to appear at Engelberg in the course of the early
years of Mount Angel's existence diminished the enthusiasm of the
motherhouse for its Oregon foundation. Father Maurus, revered as
the founding figure of Mount Angel after Fr. Adelhelm, was known
in his later years to recount how many monks in positions of influence at Engelberg in the decade after Mount Angel's founding saw
little prospect for the Oregon foundation succeeding. On a visit to
Engelberg in 1885, Abbot Frowin was asked by Abbot Anselm to take
jurisdiction over Mount Angel, but the Conception superior expressed

his reluctance to do so. At the same time, he noted that the Engelberg community's support of Mount Angel had waned considerably, with monks of the motherhouse speaking of the "debt and disorder" in Oregon.[18] In that same visit Abbot Frowin resigned himself to the fact that Engelberg would be reluctant to lend any more financial help to either of its American houses in the near future.

Given his concern with the financial state of Mount Angel, Abbot Anselm requested that Archbishop Gross be his representative in America and conduct visitations at the monastery in 1888 and 1890. There is both apprehension and frustration reflected in the journal entries of Abbot Anselm during these initial years of Mount Angel's existence. The move on his part to find a trusted third party on the scene to introduce some caution and oversight on the freewheeling maneuvers of Fr. Adelhelm is understandable. The fact that the third party would be the earlier nemesis of Fr. Adelhelm, Abbot Frowin, makes the storyline of Mount Angel's young history even more extraordinary.

At the request of Fr. Adelhelm and with the support of Abbot Anselm, Abbot Frowin made his first visit to Mount Angel in 1891. By this time, Fr. Adelhelm had begun to appreciate the wisdom and judgment of Abbot Frowin. Both Archbishop Gross and Abbot Anselm thought that another visitation of the monastery would be helpful. In 1891 the monastery was deeply in debt because of the land purchases and building expenses. Father Nicholas had left the community and there was some contention between Fr. Adelhelm and other community members. One of the observations made by Abbot Frowin in the course of the visitation was of the overwork of the fraters and brothers, resulting in the essentials of monastic practice suffering. Nonetheless, he commented on "a very good spirit inside the monastery, even if there are many things to counsel the monks about."[19] The concern about overwork would become a recurring one in subsequent years. At this stage of Mount Angel's history, however, it seemed part and parcel of the monastery's solidarity with the work ethic and endurance of the immigrant population they served.

18. Journal entry of February 3, 1885, CAA.
19. Journal entry of July 21, 1891, CAA.

The Fire of 1892

On May 3, 1892, the fortunes of the new community were changed abruptly. A fire that afternoon destroyed the monastery, church, and seminary buildings, as well as the mill and carpenter shop. Only the college building and some outlying farm structures were spared. Although there were no injuries or deaths from the blaze, the reality of the devastation was there for the students and monks to see. Insurance would cover only a small portion of the damaged buildings. The community, already in debt, now faced a new set of challenges that would take them through a crucible of sacrifice and forced adaptation.

The first challenge was to find a place for the monks and students to live. In this regard the local townspeople and the Benedictine sisters were indispensable aids. Given the fact that a new monastery would not be completed until more than ten years later in 1903, it is remarkable to consider how crucial the "temporary" residences in the town and the convent became for the monastic community and student body.[20] The sisters were especially generous in providing food service to the student body of the college and seminarians. This was only one more proof of the supportive framework that was in place early on between the Benedictine communities of men and women in Mt. Angel.

At a time when nativist sentiment toward Catholics in the Northwest and elsewhere was in the ascendant, a striking grace of the fire was the generous response given by local civic officials. The mayors of both the capital city in nearby Salem and of Portland made special appeals on behalf of the monastery. Archbishop Gross was also most supportive. After touring the charred ruins of the monastery, he made an appeal to the clergy and faithful of the archdiocese to come to the monastery's aid. The archbishop supplied another pillar of support to the community by serving as its retreat master and promoting the monastery's vital role in the spiritual health of the archdiocese.

There was no skirting the nagging reality that at the time of the fire Mount Angel had a debt of about $200,000. It was out of the question to expect that the community could pay off its debt to Engelberg, and

20. Cyril Drnjevic, OSB, "From 'Bomb' to Butte: The Establishment of Mount Angel Abbey: Part I," *American Benedictine Review* 58, no. 4 (December 2007), 427.

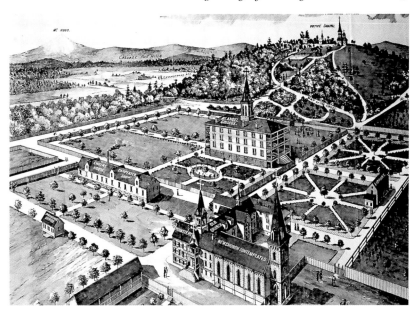

This rather idealized drawing by Br. Anselm Weissenborn was made a few days before the fire of May 3, 1892. The church on the right foreground was never built. The central building was destroyed by the fire.

that news was conveyed to Abbot Anselm. Responding in a magnanimous manner, Abbot Anselm wrote:

> When I think of their situation, consider their poverty, I must, so as not to discourage them completely and force them to disband, grant their request and try to find the help for myself from another means. If the capital is made secure in this way as a loan extension, the interest can be dispensed with for the time being. But what this enterprise in America has already cost me in worry, suffering and sleepless nights.[21]

In the aftermath of the fire there were also changes in the composition of the community leadership. Father Adelhelm, recognizing the need for funds to rebuild, committed to a "begging tour," one that would last intermittently for five years and require him to remain outside the community for most of that time. It is hard to measure whether this

21. Entry from Villiger's diary (no date given), quoted in McCrank, *Mt. Angel Abbey*, 49.

came out of any community consensus or was discerned as a practical stratagem on his part. Given the precarious character of the community's financial position, it was probably a factor in helping the morale of the monks to know that there was a concerted effort being made to search out needed sources for funds to rebuild. It did not help Fr. Adelhelm's cause that within a year the nation would undergo a serious financial panic and expected sources of aid would be compromised by their own parlous economic situation.

One of the fascinating side effects of this time away from the monastery was a steady and heartfelt correspondence Fr. Adelhelm kept with Abbot Frowin. Whatever distance and difference of opinion that may have existed when Fr. Adelhelm was in Missouri were now eclipsed by Fr. Adelhelm writing regularly to the one he addressed in his letters as "dearest spiritual father." This reconciliation seems to have antedated the fire. With the advantage of time and distance, Fr. Adelhelm had come to appreciate the leadership skills and the wisdom of Abbot Frowin and now was more than willing to tap it.

In the year after the fire, while Fr. Adelhelm was on his begging tour, Fr. Leo Huebscher became the acting prior, as well as temporary rector of the college. Nonetheless, the combination of the large debt and the absence of a strong superior on site remained an increasing concern for Engelberg.

Once again, Abbot Anselm was left with the dilemma of having no one on the scene whom he could trust for an honest accounting of what was happening at Mount Angel. To rectify this situation, Abbot Anselm decided to send one of his most trusted monks to Oregon to serve as superior in this crucial time.

The Engelberg Superior

In May of 1894, Abbot Anselm appointed Fr. Benedict Gottwald to Mount Angel as the new superior. Father Benedict was regarded as a model monk at Engelberg. He distinguished himself as the community librarian, novice master, and as a person of administrative acumen. He was to need all of that and more when he arrived in Oregon in early August of 1894. He faced a community that was not known for its monastic observance, a situation exacerbated by the dislocation of the fire. This analysis is endorsed by words that Fr. Benedict wrote soon after his arrival in early August of 1894: "It has taken me only two days to find out the sad state in which this family of the Order finds itself. . . . The whole business (the monastic observance) is not only in the material sense, but much more in the spiritual sense, greatly degenerated. There is no order, no silence, no unity . . . pure chaos."[22] It was a grim first appraisal that did not disappear anytime soon. Exacerbating the sad state of monastic observance for Fr. Benedict was what he encountered as a split between one group insistent upon maintaining Swiss traditions and another that wanted to adapt to American circumstances. It did not help that when he arrived Fr. Benedict had

Fr. Benedict Gottwald, a monk of Engelberg, was sent by Abbot Anselm Villiger to be superior for the Mount Angel Community from 1894 to 1899.

no facility in speaking English. He was to make little progress in acquiring a fluency in English in the five-year duration of his stay as superior. One indication of this is found in the minutes of the chapter meetings of the community. Up until Fr. Benedict's time they were recorded in English. For the extent of his time as superior, the chapter minutes are in German. It was only with his departure that the minutes returned to English.

There was also a clash in community sentiment over whether the new monastery should be built at the foot of the hill or on the hilltop. The discussion had pitted two differing factions of the community against each other in the years after the fire, and for a while it seemed that those who wanted to keep the monastery and school at the foot of the hill, next to the town of Mt. Angel, would hold sway. But Fr. Adelhelm was an active proponent of the monastery on the hilltop

22. Letter of Fr. Benedict Gottwald to Abbot Frowin Conrad, August 7, 1894, translated copy, MAAA.

being the best way to ensure its development as a pilgrimage spot and for the surety of a proper monastic discipline taking hold. Father Benedict was eventually brought over to Fr. Adelhelm's camp as well. It may have helped that Abbot Anselm in Engelberg also promoted the construction atop the hill for the new monastery.

Father Benedict's five years in his position as prior served as a great trial for him throughout. His own words, written a little over a year into his tenure to his close friend, Abbot Frowin, convey the crushing burden he felt: "I personally have to fight daily with the temptation to simply get up and walk away from here. The Reverend Abbot [of Engelberg] writes all the time 'Patience, patience.' However, the struggle against such conditions requires bold madness instead of patience."[23]

The letter to Conrad was one of over one hundred he wrote to his friend that constituted a revealing trove of personal exchanges between the two monastic confreres. Most of Fr. Benedict's letters can be characterized as angry in tone and critical in intent. By contrast, Abbot Frowin's letters are filled with gentle but straightforward advice, doing his best to motivate Fr. Benedict to "right the ship" and assist in bringing about the spiritual and economic health of Mount Angel.

The Conception abbot's letters reflect both his empathy for Fr. Benedict and the recognition of the distress Gottwald was experiencing at the nature of his trial:

> How deeply I feel for your situation. If I had foreseen this turn of events, I would never have been able to encourage Abbot Anselm to send you there. And yet now, more than ever, I must consider your appointment to be the work of Providence, in that I consider you the only one through whom the poor monastery may be helped, if in fact it can be helped at all. For who could unify people if not you. . . ? I pray that you may be given light, strength and perseverance; and that you may remain at Mount Angel at least until the monastery is on solid ground and secure for its future. I myself will not give up hoping that you might still come to your goal even though it may cost you great sacrifices, hard work and great patience.[24]

---

23. Letter of Fr. Benedict Gottwald to Abbot Frowin Conrad, November 28, 1895, translated copy, MAAA.

24. Letter of Abbot Frowin Conrad to Fr. Benedict Gottwald, September 27, 1894, translation by Benedict Neenan, OSB, MAAA.

The arch at the foot of the hill was the boundary for students on the hilltop.

One has an inherent sympathy for the position in which Fr. Benedict was placed. Attempting to bring about a return to monastic observance under the conditions of monks living outside the cloister was problematic enough. But added to that was the daily reminder of outstanding debts and the contending differences of community members on a variety of issues. This is illustrated by a seemingly abrupt decision of some of the Mount Angel monks in 1896 to associate themselves with the American Cassinese Congregation, a grouping of monasteries that were closely associated with German Benedictine roots, quite in contrast to the Swiss-American Congregation that had been established in 1881 and to which the communities of Conception and St. Meinrad were attached. How serious the Mount Angel community was in their intent to do this is still in question. The fact that they chose to adopt the Beuronese habit is one indication of their solidarity with the Swiss-Americans, as that was the habit the Congregation had taken on.[25]

The despondency, if not depression, that seemed to settle into Fr. Benedict's resigned mode of governance is increasingly evident in his correspondence. "To have to preside over a community with trust one does not have," he wrote to Abbot Frowin in August of 1898,

25. Father Adelhelm was in the forefront of the move to adopt the Beuronese habit. The formal confirmation of admission to the Swiss-American Congregation came in a letter from Abbot Anselm to Mount Angel in July of 1898.

"makes all the efforts lame."[26] In an even darker mood he wrote plaintively in early 1899: "Please come here in person and try to help, but I am sure you have as little desire to come as I have to remain here. I did not make profession to a house of fools."[27] Abbot Frowin laid out an alternative view of the crucial character of Fr. Benedict's role: "You know better than I the present condition of Mt. Angel and the consequences of your leaving there now. Do you really want all to be lost along with the heavy sacrifice of your five-year exile? Do not leave untried what might serve this monastery for which the Reverend Father [Anselm Villiger] has sacrificed so much."[28]

Father Benedict did write in detail and in differing moods of distress to Abbot Anselm. He described the laxity of a number of monks in attendance at Divine Office and the administrative challenge of dealing with the large burden of debt, along with the contending voices of monks who "made their own way."[29] When Fr. Benedict described Mount Angel to Abbot Frowin as "the painful child,"[30] one can intuit just how much distress the interim superior had internalized in the course of his time in Oregon.

Viewed from a larger historical framework, Fr. Benedict Gottwald was the monastic buffer that Mount Angel required in the crucial period after the fire of 1892. While the frustration experienced by Fr. Benedict in trying to implement a more monastic form of observance and a more conscious witness of financial restraint was the recurring bane of his personal life, his tenure as superior did have a plus side. It allowed time for Fr. Adelhelm to secure some added funding for the fire-devastated community on his begging trip to the eastern reaches of the United States. In doing so, it adeptly utilized Fr. Adelhelm's gifts

26. Letter of Fr. Benedict Gottwald to Abbot Frowin Conrad, August 23, 1898, translated copy in MAAA.

27. Letter of Fr. Benedict Gottwald to Abbot Frowin Conrad, March 8, 1899, translated copy in MAAA.

28. Letter of Abbot Frowin Conrad to Fr. Benedict Gottwald, January 14, 1898, translated copy in MAAA.

29. Letter of Fr. Benedict Gottwald to Abbot Anselm Villiger, August 18, 1894, translated copy, in MAAA.

30. Letter of Fr. Benedict Gottwald to Abbot Frowin, May 10, 1898, translated copy in MAAA.

of preaching and his boundless energy in a section of the country that knew little of the remote Oregon Benedictine house. His absence from the Mount Angel community for the first time in ten years permitted other monks in the community to exercise their styles of leadership.[31] Overall, it allowed members of a monastic community, that by most accounts was fractious and reeling from the devastation of a fire, time to discuss their differences and regroup as they looked to the future.

Personal contacts made by Fr. Adelhelm on his trip were impressive. He was given hospitality at the cathedral in Baltimore by Cardinal James Gibbons, and he met in Philadelphia with Mother Katherine Drexel. He also made the acquaintance of Benedictine superiors in the eastern part of the United States, such as Abbot and Vicar Apostolic Leo Haid of Belmont Abbey, North Carolina. Prior to these encounters, most of these leaders had little knowledge of what Mount Angel was and where it was located. Father Adelhelm found German-speaking areas in St. Louis, Cincinnati, and Newark to be especially fruitful in their giving. Through 1893, Fr. Adelhelm was able to collect enough money to sustain Mount Angel in its day-to-day operations, but not enough to defray the large debt. When the devastating nature of the Panic of 1893 took hold in 1894, he made the prudent decision to return home to Oregon and work from Sacred Heart Parish in Portland, only to make another excursion to the eastern part of the country at the end of the decade.

One notable move made by Fr. Benedict, one that was to establish a precedent that had long-lasting positive effects for the community, was to send younger monks for their advanced theological studies to Europe. In Rome, the international house of studies for Benedictines, Sant'Anselmo, had just been established on the Aventine Hill. It was to Sant'Anselmo that Fr. Benedict in 1895 sent Frater Jerome Wespe (Swiss-born) and Frater Bernard Murphy (an American-born native of Portland) to the "Anselmianum," grateful for the assurance from the Abbot Primate that their costs for enrollment and education would be covered. Both Wespe and Murphy were to play key roles in the early

---

31. Although Fr. Leo Huebscher's time as prior (before Fr. Benedict) and sub-prior was not particularly fruitful, the appointment of a young Fr. Maurus Snyder as subprior was an example of younger leadership from the ranks.

history of Mount Angel, and they brought back to Oregon a widened vision of monasticism that was to be copied by many other monks sent to Europe in the following decades. It is revealing that during their time in Europe, Fr. Adelhelm took the initiative in writing on a regular basis to Fraters Bernard and Jerome. He clearly saw them as the future leaders in the community, and he did all he could to promote their monastic formation. Indeed, when Fr. Bernard returned home from Rome in the autumn of 1899, he was given permission by Fr. Adelhelm to reside at Conception Abbey to write his doctoral dissertation. What had once been described by Fr. Adelhelm as a Beuronese betrayal of Engelberg was now extolled as a "model of peace and recollection" under "holy and learned" Abbot Frowin.[32] Truly the perspective of Fr. Adelhelm had undergone a transformation from the time he had left Missouri in 1881.

For all the criticism leveled against the monastery by Fr. Benedict and others in the difficult years after the fire, there remained a core group of monks that was resolute in their determination to forge a genuine Benedictine community. This resolve is exemplified in a letter written by Fr. Dominic Weadenschwyler in 1896 to confreres at Engelberg:

> I tell you candidly that I sustain myself only with the hope that one day we too shall have a monastery in which the true spirit of St. Benedict prevails according to or even in union with the best formed Benedictine congregation in Europe. If anyone would take this hope out of my heart I would be wretched and completely unhappy.[33]

It was unfortunate that this underlying determination to become a monastery that reflected the best elements of European models was undercut by the practical demands of financial survival and the contending visions present in the community during these years. This internal division was registered in a number of areas. There was the previously mentioned divide between monks who wanted to rebuild the monastery and the school at the base of the hilltop and others who

32. Letter of Fr. Adelhelm to Fr. Bernard Murphy, November 22, 1889, MAAA.
33. Letter of Fr. Dominic Weadenschwyler to Engelberg, March 20, 1896, translated copy in MAAA.

The building on the left is the Queen of Angels monastery of the Benedictine sisters. On the right is the Mount Angel Academy for women.

wanted to remove everything to the top of the hill. There was another emerging division between "school monks," who put a priority on the educational apostolate and those monks who believed the primary interest of the community was to foster a sound internal spiritual life. There also remained the tension between those who wanted to retain Swiss customs and the German language and those who saw a need for greater assimilation and adjustment to American culture.

By 1898 there was some resolution to the conflicted currents at work in the monastery. On April 4 the community decided to erect a permanent monastery on the hilltop. This represented an avenue for the future that would have a decidedly positive impact on the community's fortunes. It was a vindication of the vision of Fr. Adelhelm, the stated conviction of Abbot Anselm and Archbishop Gross, and a signal of the new purpose present in the community. From the moment of this decision, the center of Mount Angel's future would be on the forty-six acres at the top of the hill.

In all of this, Abbot Anselm maintained his commitment to the struggling foundation. His prudent counsel and consistent pledge of support carried his American charges through their roughest stretches. Amazingly enough, he performed something of the same function for Sr. Bernadine Wachter in her capacity as superior for the women of Queen of Angels Monastery in the town of Mt. Angel and for the Swiss

Benedictine sisters from Sarnen, who made a foundation in Idaho.[34] The advocacy of Abbot Anselm, in the face of the many crises he was required to manage, made the topic of survival for these Benedictine communities in Oregon and Idaho far less dire in its character.

A Transition in Leadership

The other event in 1898 that had significant influence on the future of Mount Angel was the decision of the chapter at Engelberg on August 14 to place the community of Mount Angel under the canonical jurisdiction of Abbot Frowin Conrad of Conception Abbey. This was a decision precipitated by an extraordinary request made by the monastic chapter of Mount Angel to Abbot Anselm in early 1898, one that merits quoting in detail:

> We know only one way that would help us out of this difficult situation and lead us to a good end. How grateful we would be to you, Rev. Father and Abbot, if you would assist us to this step. We ask your Reverence . . . to have the Rev. Father and Abbot Frowin appointed to be administrator of our monastery with *all rights* and *duties* and with the entire responsibility of an Abbot, and this at least for as long as our present predicament persists. Our unstable existence, thereby, would be made safe and the present difficulties would be smoothed over. The Rev. Father Abbot Frowin, at his last stay here, captured the love, respect and good will of all Capitulars. . . . If, in this way, the entire supervision of our community were in the hands of the Rev. Father Abbot Frowin, then for the office of Prior a more qualified person than Rev. Father Adelhelm Odermatt could hardly be found. Under the personal direction of these two men of God the work would have to thrive and flourish.[35]

At first glance there is prescience in this directive that is arresting. To think that a community, one that had begun its existence as an alternative to the monastic model of Abbot Frowin at Conception and that had

---

34. See Evangela Bossert, "From Swiss Cloister to American Frontier: The Early History of the Benedictine Sisters of Idaho," *American Benedictine Review* 58, no. 4 (December 2007), 396.

35. Petition of Mount Angel Capitulars to Abbot Anselm Villiger, March 28, 1898, translation by Jim Dunn, MAAA.

railed against the impulsive decision making of Fr. Adelhelm, could
now recommend both of them as
a necessary leadership team challenges the logical flow of Mount
Angel's narrative.

This constituted a role reversal
in multiple ways. Abbot Anselm,
the superior who had once rep-
rimanded Abbot Frowin for his
implementation of non-Engelberg
practices, now was to fully endorse
him as the one person most capable of salvaging Mount Angel's
shaky monastic beginnings. Abbot
Frowin, the person who in many
ways had prompted Fr. Adelhelm's
odyssey of starting a "New Engelberg," was now given authority to
rescue it from its struggle for financial survival and prompt the

Abbot Frowin Conrad played an
indispensable role as spiritual father
for the Mount Angel community from
1899 to 1919.

establishment of regular monastic observance. To that end of establishing regular monastic observance, Abbot Frowin conducted an exhaus-
tive visitation in 1898 that lasted almost a month. It was this visitation
that prompted the capitulars' endearing phrase of how Abbot Frowin
captured their love and respect. In his journal, Abbot Frowin gave voice
to his reaction to the visitation and certainly affirms that he was not
looking at the community through rose-colored glasses: "Under the
pretext that everything at Mount Angel should be as in Engelberg, it
seems the community went to an extreme. They put too much reliance
on the abuses of Engelberg and did not embrace Engelberg's good customs. . . . There are also those who are set against Engelberg, a possible consequence of the earlier poor administration of Mount Angel."[36]

What strikes the observer of all the important players in Mount Angel's early history is that Abbot Frowin was the person most respected

36. Translation of Journal entry of November 24, 1898, CAA.

and recognized as the one individual singularly capable of bringing about unity and a healthy monastic spirit for the Oregon monks. Father Adelhelm, the one-time adversary of Abbot Frowin, was now on record as telling Abbot Anselm that Conrad's leadership was essential for Mount Angel's growth. Father Benedict Gottwald expressed his unequivocal confidence in Conrad's ability to bring about the cohesion of the community that he had so laboriously tried to effect in his five years as superior,[37] no doubt wishing that the appointment of Abbot Frowin had come sooner. There was yet another twist in leadership roles. Upon Fr. Benedict's departure for Engelberg in 1899, Fr. Adelhelm was appointed as prior yet again, but now serving under the canonical authority of Abbot Frowin. The deference that was firmly in place toward Abbot Frowin is reflected in words that Fr. Adelhelm wrote to him shortly after the appointment: "I am very grateful for your good and best fatherly advice, and I know your perfect intentions and I always will be glad to receive your *correctio fraterna* any time, openly and plainly."[38]

The service rendered by Fr. Benedict as prior of Mount Angel officially came to a close on June 13, 1899. On that day at a chapter meeting, a letter was read from Abbot Anselm, announcing his release of Fr. Benedict from his duties at Mount Angel in response to Fr. Benedict's repeated wishes and in concern for his health.[39] At the same chapter a letter was read from Fr. Benedict thanking the community for the good will they had shown during his years in office and asking forgiveness for his own shortcomings. Abbot Anselm's concern for Fr. Benedict's health was more than just a pretext for his release. He returned to Engelberg visibly worn by the experience and never recaptured the energy and drive he had shown prior to his being sent to Mount Angel, dying within the decade of his return to Switzerland. A last directive from Abbot Anselm at the June 13 chapter was the formal

---

37. There is an extensive correspondence between Conrad and Gottwald, especially in the latter's time as prior of Mount Angel, 1894–99. In many respects, Gottwald was willing to remain at Mount Angel only because of the strong urging of Conrad, MAAA.

38. Letter of Adelhelm Odermatt to Abbot Frowin Conrad, July 11, 1899, CAA.

39. Chapter minutes of June 13, 1899, MAAA.

reappointment of Fr. Adelhelm as prior, with the request that the community show him all respect and submission.[40] Abbot Anselm could more securely ask for that respect for his prior, knowing that the higher authority of oversight and direction would be held by Abbot Frowin.

The ultimate jurisdiction wielded by Abbot Frowin was conditioned by the physical distance between Conception and Mount Angel and Conrad's primary duties as abbot of his monastery and as abbot president of the Swiss-American Congregation. Nonetheless, the Conception superior gave Mount Angel a direction and vision it had previously lacked. It was under the aegis of the Conception superior that Mount Angel reaffirmed its intention to operate as a member of the Swiss-American Congregation of monks. It was also Abbot Frowin who oversaw the first election of a superior at Mount Angel and its erection as an abbey.

Independence and a New Superior

The death of Abbot Anselm Villiger of Engelberg on January 15, 1901 marked a new and telling transition for the Mount Angel community. Father Leodegar Scherr was elected to succeed Villiger. Abbot Leodegar had been a monk working in the college at Engelberg in the early 1880s when Fr. Adelhelm had made his aggressive push to attract students from there to his new venture in America. Like many of his Swiss confreres, he had witnessed the increasing costs incurred by Engelberg in support of the Oregon foundation. He had most likely heard of Fr. Benedict's negative evaluation of the community upon his return to Engelberg in 1899.

One of the first official acts of the new abbot was to write Abbot Frowin and confirm his position as the representative of Engelberg with jurisdiction over Mount Angel. Pursuant to that role, Abbot Frowin was instructed to conduct a canonical visitation of Mount Angel, one that would emphatically convey to the Mount Angel monks the Engelberg abbot's wish to see the community stay a member of the Swiss-American Congregation, initiate a more thorough financial accounting, and conduct an election for a new superior. Abbot Frowin, ever the

40. Chapter minutes of June 13, 1899, MAAA.

The photo shows the monastic community and dignitaries gathered for the blessing of Mount Angel's first abbot, Thomas Meienhofer, June 29, 1904.

obedient monk, proceeded to conduct the visitation, along with giving a three-day retreat to the community. The result of all this was the election, after a long succession of ballots, of Fr. Thomas Meienhofer as the new prior of Mount Angel on July 11, 1901. The election results were pleasing to Abbot Leodegar, since Prior Thomas had been a student of Scherr's at Engelberg and a mentor for the younger man as he became a priest and monk at Engelberg.

Changes of superior frequently became turning points in the history of religious communities. At this juncture in Mount Angel's development, a new chemistry was in evidence. Father Adelhelm was chastised by Abbot Leodegar for his importunate request for possibly more loans of money, in the form of an untactful aside that came in a letter congratulating Abbot Leodegar on his election. The new Engelberg abbot let it be known that Fr. Adelhelm was no longer setting the tone for the Oregon house's mission and future. No doubt both Abbot Leodegar and the monks of Mount Angel were in agreement that a new course was needed with a new person at the helm.

A positive change of venue for the monastery took place in the fall of 1903 when the monastic community, the seminarians, and college students all moved into their new living quarters on the hilltop. Alexander Christie, the archbishop of Portland, continued to send men to the seminary, and that assured a solid core of students at a time when some observers questioned the viability of the "Little Seminary." Contrary to the negative forecasts of some critics of the seminary, its enrollment slowly rose to a total of 36 students in 1909. So, too, the monastery could now enjoy the quiet and physical detachment of the hilltop, a setting more conducive to Benedictine life.

Three years after the 1901 visitation and election, Abbot Frowin directed another visitation and another election. Since the community now wanted to advance to an independent abbatial status, the new superior would most likely become the first abbot of Mount Angel. A vote was taken on February 3. After nine ballots, the result was the election of Fr. Prior Thomas as abbot. He was approved by Rome as the first abbot of Mount Angel on March 23, 1904. Mount Angel officially became an abbey on the following day, March 24. Abbot Thomas was blessed at a ceremony on June 29, 1904. In the absence of Archbishop Christie of Portland who was ill, Abbot Frowin was the presiding prelate, assisted by Abbot Athanasius Schmitt of St. Meinrad and Abbot Vincent Wehrle of St. Mary's Abbey in North Dakota. In attendance were a number of bishops and the governor of Oregon, George Chamberlain. Abbot Leodegar signaled his positive response to this news by sending to Abbot Thomas a pectoral cross from Engelberg and the diocesan clergy presented the new abbot with a crosier from the Benziger Brothers.

In a terse statement with injected irony in his journal, Abbot Frowin provided an editorial comment on what had transpired when he wrote: "How could I have imagined in the year 1881, with the departure of Fathers Adelhelm and Nicholas, which caused me so much grief, that I would be called to administer the blessing of the first abbot of Mt. Angel."[41] What Abbot Frowin did not add but what could have been surmised by members of the Mount Angel community in 1904 was that if anyone had earned the right to the title of spiritual father of the community at this stage in their story, it would be Abbot Frowin Conrad before any of their own members.

41. Journal entry of June 6, 1904, CAA.

CHAPTER THREE

An Independent Enterprise

Composition of the Community

B Y 1900, the monks in the Mount Angel community were forty-five in number. There was more than twice the number of lay brothers to monk-priests. While the contingent of priest-monks who performed the major part of the parish supply work in the first two decades of Mount Angel's history were largely drawn from Engelberg, the new membership drew largely from the local population. The overwhelming ethnic makeup was from German and Swiss family heritage. Most of these monks, in turn, came from farming families that were familiar with the manual labor that would be required of the pioneer period of the community history.

The fact that lay brothers constituted the majority of membership in early years is not surprising. This was also the case with other Benedictine communities founded in the United States in the nineteenth century. The reality of the demands made on these communities was of a considerable manual workforce that would provide a stable presence in the monastery precincts, even as many of the priest-monks were called to serve parishes outside the monastery proper and fraters or monks who were preparing for priesthood were sent away for study. There was a further distinction seen in lay brothers who had come from Switzerland and those who had entered from America. The Swiss lay brothers were aware that they were not included as members of the chapter of the community and did not take solemn vows or have an active voice in such things as the election of a superior. They readily accepted this as part of their call. The Americans who entered as lay brothers did not entirely share in those expectations. This is reflected in a letter written by Fr. Adelhelm to Abbot Fintan Mundwiler of St. Meinrad in 1888: "There would be an uproar if I do not promise the American lay brothers solemn vows."[1] That expectation of full membership in the monastic community would not be fulfilled until eighty years later. However, for the crucial time frame of the founding generation, the lay brothers were to provide a hands-on investment in the agricultural and maintenance aspects of community life, a role that served as an indispensable ingredient for Mount Angel's continued growth. In this the lay brothers found themselves in a similar situation to their counterparts in the world of American Benedictines, having a separate prayer chapel, a modified Divine Office and social separation from the rest of the community.

A Troubled Tenure

The tenure of Abbot Thomas was one that reprised some earlier themes. There was a recurring effort to bring about better monastic discipline and stricter financial accountability, a hope that was foremost in the expectation of Abbot Leodegar and the community at Engelberg. A review of the correspondence of Abbot Thomas in the period after he was installed as abbot reveals someone who saw himself as a reformer. He wrote in 1905: "A reformer's life is along hard lines; he, as a rule, runs no risks of being drowned in an ocean of love and affection. But never mind he has the chance to make even Priors sweat when he hauls them over the coals."[2] There was no observable honeymoon period or ocean of affection that was visible in the hilltop community. The acerbic coda to the abbot's letter reflects another constant in his correspondence, a cavalier and critical attitude toward his monks. Father Jerome Wespe wrote to Abbot Frowin in 1906 to let him know that he could no longer function as novice master because of how practices in the house at Mount Angel were at cross-purposes with his teaching.

---

1. Letter of Fr. Adelhelm Odermatt to Abbot Fintan Mundwiler, April 6, 1888, translated copy in Mount Angel Abbey Archives (hereafter MAAA).

2. Letter of Abbot Thomas Meienhofer to Abbot Frowin Conrad, March 6, 1905, Archives of Conception Abbey (hereafter CAA).

Fathers Berthold Durrer and Gregory Robl also wrote to Abbot Frowin, expressing their frustration with the leadership performance of their abbot. When Abbot Frowin reported to Abbot Thomas instances of the unrest and complaints on the part of Mount Angel monks that had written to him, Abbot Thomas became testy and combative: "Ingratitude and difficulties of every possible description have well nigh broken me. It would indeed take very little to make me turn overboard my burden for we can bear only to a certain limit . . . these and a million other things have truly disgusted me and have almost undermined my faith."[3] From 1906 on, the letters of Abbot Thomas are filled with self-pity and suspicion, bordering on paranoia. Some of this was no doubt the residue of his volatile and overly defensive interactions with individual monks. He clearly alienated more than a few of his confreres with his dismissive manner. When his declining physical health was added to this condition, it is easy to see how the abbot detached himself increasingly from community life. It is difficult to discern how much of the recurring complaint of his intestinal problems was real and how much psychosomatic. The fact that he connected his stomach distress with his vision problems leads one to consider an admixture of job stress and hypochondria as factors contributing to his growing alienation from the community.

Throughout all of this, Abbot Frowin continued to serve as a mentor, model, and corrector to the Mount Angel abbot. An example of this can be seen in 1908. That September Abbot Frowin conducted a visitation and was perplexed at having Abbot Thomas leave the abbey for Portland and not return for several days. He also expressed disappointment that during the subsequent retreat a number of the monks were absent. Nonetheless, Abbot Frowin returned by train to St. Meinrad Abbey in the company of Abbot Thomas for the General Chapter of the Swiss-American Congregation, after which he encouraged Abbot Thomas to visit the other abbeys of the Congregation.[4] Abbot Frowin was also interlocutor with members of the abbey who had difficulty accepting the

---

3. Letter of Abbot Thomas Meienhofer to Abbot Frowin Conrad, May 14, 1908, CAA.

4. *Abbey Chronicle*, VIII, p. 6. The *Abbey Chronicle* is a collection of historical reflections by year written by Fr. Martin Pollard, originally appearing in the *Mount Angel Letter* and now collected in a bound volume in MAAA.

The front of the Benedictine Press and Post Office, circa 1910.

governance style and decisions of Abbot Thomas. The one obstacle to assisting efforts at bringing the newly independent community the wise outside counsel Abbot Frowin afforded was the distance of Conception, Missouri, from Mount Angel, Oregon. Given the multi-day trip by train that it took Abbot Frowin to come to Oregon, along with his substantial duties as abbot of his own monastery and the abbot president of his congregation, it was impractical to expect that he could provide the oversight and monastic formation that the superiors in Engelberg had hoped for and that Mount Angel clearly needed at this time.

There were other positions that were filled in the Mount Angel community under Abbot Thomas. Father Adelhelm was named prior for a third time. As he aged, Fr. Adelhelm became less the gruff and hard-driving superior and more the pliant and peaceable elder, eager to forge a degree of unity. One of the new abbot's better appointments was placing Fr. Dominic Waedenschwyler as head of the college. At the same time, Fr. Dominic maintained a pastoral presence in both the Native American mission outposts and local parishes and contributed to the musical resources of the abbey. The position of novice and junior master fell to two of the younger members of the community, Fr. Jerome Wespe and later Fr. Bernard Murphy. Although both men were not always in agreement with the abbot's model of monastic formation, the fact that two future leaders of the community were selected to fill that important position speaks well of the judgment of Abbot Thomas.

Abbot Thomas deserves credit for his support of the publications associated with Mount Angel. The Benedictine Press, begun on a small scale in 1889, began to make new strides in the new century. In 1900 it purchased a German newspaper weekly, *St. Josephs Blatt.* For many German-American Catholics, the adage "the language saves the faith" was a deeply internalized belief and in taking that phrase as its motto the Press saw itself in the

Br. Celestine Mueller, manager of the Benedictine Press and editor of the *St. Josephs Blatt.*

forefront of that effort. In the early 1900s it could point to 50,000 subscribers, a number that was further augmented when the weekly acquired North Dakota and Philadelphia German-Catholic newspapers, and its coverage became nationwide and not just local.[5] In 1900 the *Mt. Angel Magazine* began a long publishing history. It morphed after several decades into *St. Joseph Magazine,* another Catholic periodical intended for a wide audience. To foster the growth of these publications, a new and enlarged Benedictine Press building was constructed and finished in 1909. In that same year Br. Celestine Mueller was named as director of the Press. By this time the Press was recognized as a valued revenue producer and public voice for the community. In this it was in a long line of Benedictine tradition that used the printed word as a channel for evangelization and education.

5. Lawrence McCrank, *Mt. Angel Abbey: A Centennial History of the Benedictine Community and Its Library, 1882–1982* (Wilmington, DE: Scholarly Resources, 1983), 61.

Photo from within the Press of the mailing of the weekly German-language
St. Josephs Blatt.

As it was with so many of the figures in Mount Angel's early history, there was a regular correspondence between Abbot Thomas and Abbot Frowin. It reveals how the Mount Angel superior showed increasing signs of bitterness and resentment toward monks in the Mount Angel community who disagreed with what Abbot Thomas described as his "reform efforts."[6] Although Abbot Frowin tried his best to mediate these differences as part of his role as abbot president and friend, it became evident that rifts between the abbot and monks were deepening, with the result that, with respect to the daily life of the monastery, it was left to the monks of the community to decide on administrative decisions and even assigned work.

About five years after his election, Abbot Thomas began to experience health problems. The most disturbing of these was a loss of vision in his right eye. It seemed to be connected to some intestinal problems that also emerged. In his last two years as superior (1908–10), Abbot

---

6. Letters in CAA show Abbot Frowin having to deal with increasingly querulous comments on Mount Angel monks by Abbot Thomas, along with a series of formal protests from the monks of Mount Angel addressed to Abbot Frowin.

Thomas had to absent himself from the community for extended periods of time to receive medical attention for his condition. These protracted periods of time the abbot spent in Portland away from the community were a source of comment and concern among other community members. Even though the community had a parish in Portland, Sacred Heart, Abbot Thomas was never known to stop there during his stays in the city. Much to the consternation of the monks in Mount Angel, Abbot Thomas was unreachable during his stays in Portland. The monks were also plagued with questions from the clergy of Portland asking where the abbot was and why he did not show himself.[7]

Three community members felt compelled to send a letter to Abbot Frowin in 1909, decrying the absence of Abbot Thomas from the community and the scandal it invited. They added: "Financial oversight is non-existent . . . by back-biting, detraction and serious slander the community was set at variance."[8] The criticism grew in the first months of 1910, with hints of how financial impropriety and theological modernism connected to the person of the abbot were creating scandal among some of the faithful. The fact that Fr. Jerome supported some of these criticisms reveals that by this time the resistance in the community was not limited to what Abbot Thomas had referred to as the malcontents. Abbot Thomas reserved some of his harshest criticism for his prior, Fr. Adelhelm. Curiously, he claimed the monks were taking advantage of the abbot's long periods away from the monastery to receive what he perceived as overly lenient permissions from Fr. Adelhelm.

Abbot Thomas was absent from the monastery about 80 percent of the time from November of 1909 through April of 1910. Few matters of consequence could be dealt with at the abbey as a result. One can also detect a bitterness among the monks of the abbey over the contentious and biting judgments that Abbot Thomas openly rendered in his last years as abbot. There seemed to be no common ground that the abbot and the community could occupy. Any objective assessment given by an outsider looking at the abbey in May of 1910 would likely characterize it as dysfunctional.

7. Letter of Fr. Berthold Durrer to Abbot Frowin, March 11, 1910, MAAA.

8. Letter of Frs. Berthold, Gregory, and Joseph to Abbot Frowin, Dec. 18, 1909, MAAA.

Still, it came as a surprise for many of the Mount Angel chapter members to receive word that Abbot Thomas submitted by letter his resignation on May 25, 1910, effective on that date. He wrote the letter to Fr. Adelhelm, his prior, where he aptly summarized his reasoning: "I have made up my mind to go in quest of health while it is still time. But I cannot freely do so as long as I hold my position as Abbot of St. Benedict's Abbey. To do so would wrong the Abbey, the chapter and myself. The Abbey must be guided by a healthy man who can stand the work and the strain. I can do so no longer. The patience of the chapter has been tried to the limit. I do not blame anyone for becoming restless; I think I owe the chapter an apology for staying in office so long after I realized that I could not attend to my duties in a satisfactory manner."[9]

Unprepared as the community was to receive this news, a further shock came when it was discovered that their superior had left the community in the company of a woman and traveled to Chicago.[10] In the meantime, the Mount Angel monks were required to wait for the ratification of the resignation from both the president of the Swiss-American Congregation (Abbot Frowin) and church officials in Rome. There followed an unsettled period of several months when the monastery had to field queries about the whereabouts of their former abbot and the future of their leadership. It was decidedly a difficult time for the monks of Mount Angel, both in terms of their internal peace and their relations with the world around them. Reports in the local press of the departure of Abbot Thomas, with details of the divorced woman, a familiar figure in Portland high society, whom he had been said to have married, became another irritant to community peace. Father Gregory Robl, writing to Abbot Frowin with enclosures of some of the newspaper stories, summarized the feeling: "I hope that by joint prayer this scandal be soon forgotten. The archbishop is indignant and so are the priests. I send you this that you may see that we were

9. Letter of Abbot Thomas Meienhofer to Fr. Adelhelm Odermatt, May 25, 1910, CAA.

10. The ensuing history of Thomas (Francis) Meienhofer is part melodrama and enigma. He eventually settled in New York City, a move verified by a front-page photo and story in the tabloid *New York World* of May 15, 1911. He maintained contact with a number of people connected to Mount Angel in ensuing years, principally Fr. Maurus Snyder. He married and lived with his wife until his death in Virginia on September 6, 1936.

The monks occupied this "second monastery" from December 24, 1903, to
September 20, 1926.

conscientious in reporting that monstrosity of a superior to you for
the good of monks and religious."[11] The repercussions of the abrupt
departure of Abbot Thomas and the notoriety about the abbey that it
left in his wake are not easy to measure, but it is safe to say that they
weighed heavily on the collective identity of the community for years
to come. The collective resilience and spiritual mettle of the monks of
Mount Angel were tried in new ways.

Some of the anxiety and apprehension present in the community
in this time are found in a letter sent by Fr. Bernard Murphy to Abbot
Frowin. Father Bernard had made efforts as both novice master and
subprior under Abbot Thomas to improve the level of monastic observance, but the assessment he gives of life in the community in July
of 1910 is sobering:

> Most of our men have no idea of religious life left. The spirit of the
> world has occupied everything. Benedictine ideals are laughed at or
> entirely ignored. There are but four of us who arise in the morning for
> Lauds, and these same men are the only ones who make a meditation.
> Of course, you can easily imagine what influence such manner of acting
> has on the Fraters and Brothers. And the drink evil is worse than ever. I
> beseech you dear Father Abbot, help us to get a good, zealous Superior

11. Letter of Fr. Gregory Robl to Abbot Frowin, March 23, 1911. The newspaper
in question was the *Oregon Journal* of March 22, 1911, CAA.

who can remedy these terrible abuses. Poor Abbot Thomas was rarely at home; so they [the abuses] grew up in his absence. Good Father Prior [Adelhelm] expects to be elected; but he is the *wrong man*, much more now than ten years ago. He is personally a good man; we are very good friends; but the way he gives useless permissions, throws out money, and the way Fathers absent themselves from choir for months—all this shows that he is not the right man for Abbot. Father Jerome [Wespe] is thoroughly disgusted and told me that he will have nothing to do with things if Father Prior gets in. . . . I know I must strike my breast and say *Mea Culpa* for the way I have allowed the Novices and Clerics liberties this past year. For three years I had strictly forbidden them any relations with the students in any way. I was criticized and called a tyrant for doing so, even Father Abbot deeming me too strict; so I allowed them to take part in athletics this last year. That taught me such a lesson that I will not soon forget.[12]

The "lesson" for Fr. Bernard was that there needed to be a certain strictness in the formation of monks, lest license enter in. It is also evident when reading Fr. Bernard's analysis that the turbulent nature of community life at Mount Angel during the abbacy of Abbot Thomas was carrying on beyond his departure. No doubt Abbot Frowin appreciated the assessment of Fr. Adelhelm's leadership potential given by Fr. Bernard, as well as the need for better monastic discipline.

In the uncertain interim of months after the departure of Abbot Thomas, Prior Adelhelm served as administrator of the

Photo of Abbot Placidus Fuerst shortly after his election in 1910.

12. Letter of Fr. Bernard Murphy to Abbot Frowin Conrad, July 26, 1910, copy in CAA.

community and did his best to maintain some return to a normal rhythm of monastic life. Finally, on August 30, 1910, under the authority of Abbot Frowin, an election was held and Fr. Placidus Fuerst was chosen as the second abbot of Mount Angel. The formal blessing of Abbot Placidus took place on October 5, with Abbot Frowin presiding.

A Time of Growth and Testing

Abbot Placidus was a monk of manifest gifts. German-born, he was an accomplished musician who continued to play the organ for abbey liturgies after he was abbot. He had taught in the Mount Angel schools from 1888–93 and was director of the college in the difficult years after the fire (1893–99). He was the first of the Mount Angel monks to do his theological study at the Catholic University of America. In 1901 he was made pastor of St. Mary's Church in Mt. Angel and oversaw the construction of a new church edifice in the years prior to his election as abbot. He inherited a community that was still feeling the strains of his successor's unexpected departure and of some lingering divisions. He expressed his intent to try and make a more cohesive monastic community and to continue the pastoral outreach of the monastery. To that end he appointed as the new prior Fr. Maurus Snyder, whom he recalled from the Native American mission on Vancouver Island at the Christie School.[13] Father Maurus served the community well as second in command.

As had been the case with his predecessors as superior, Abbot Placidus looked to Abbot Frowin for guidance and support. A little over a year into his tenure in office, Abbot Placidus felt overwhelmed by some of the challenges he faced and offered his resignation to Abbot Frowin. The abbot president refused to accept the resignation and encouraged him to continue to discharge his duties with a firm hand.[14]

13. He took over the job as prior on September 1, 1911, *Abbey Chronicle* IX, 6. Father Maurus, the first novice and the first priest to be ordained at Mount Angel, is also in many ways the first historian of the community. His research and writing on the beginnings of Mount Angel remain valuable components of its early history.

14. Journal entry of November 21, 1911, CAA.

Abbot Frowin made a point of corresponding with Abbot Placidus in the months that followed, giving him personal support and wise counsel. Coming to Mount Angel in August of 1912, Abbot Frowin arranged a new set of monastic regulations "to remove some abuses." He also encouraged an exchange of community members that were studying theology at Conception and Mount Angel.

Abbot Placidus was able to preserve the peace of his community in a decade that presented him with a host of challenges. He maintained good relations with the Benedictine women of Queen of Angels Convent, helped by the fact that his own sibling, Sr. Beatrice, was a member of that community. Having had experience in both the schools and parish work, he had the respect of his monks in making appointments and overseeing the monastery's ministries. He appointed Fr. Dominic Waedenschwyler, a fellow monastic musician, to take his place as pastor in the parish in the town of Mt. Angel and was pleased to see the new church dedicated on June 30, 1912. He wrote to his prior during the first year of his tenure that he wanted to transform the abbey into a "model community." He felt he had the priest-monks on his side in doing this but did not have the brothers and those on the farm behind him.[15] That remained a challenge for the course of his time as abbot.

Mention should be made of the practice begun by Fr. Benedict Gottwald and continued by Abbot Placidus that became an essential ingredient to Mount Angel's monastic maturity—sending its young monks to Europe for study. Building upon the positive experience undergone by Fathers Bernard Murphy and Jerome Wespe in Rome, Abbot Placidus in turn sent Fraters Bede Rose and Victor Rassier to Sant'Anselmo for theological studies in 1913. This was just prior to the start of World War I. Many more monks were to follow in their footsteps, and it would redound to the benefit of the monastic community, the students at Mount Angel, and many others. It did not seem an accident that the majority of subsequent superiors and formation personnel in the house were those who were given the benefit of a European education and cultural experience.

15. Letter of Abbot Placidus Fuerst to Fr. Maurus Snyder, October 28, 1910, translation, MAAA.

Photo of the monastic community in 1915. At center are Abbot Frowin Conrad, flanked by Abbot Placidus and Fr. Adelhelm.

Abbot Frowin conducted a visitation of the community in August of 1911 and gave positive reports back to Engelberg. He also joined Abbot Placidus in attending the Congress of Abbots in Rome in September of 1913 and, to solidify the bonds with Engelberg, Abbot Placidus made a visit to Switzerland for the first time since he had left Engelberg in 1882.[16]

Another abbot entered the picture in an honorary way on September 29, 1916. That was the date of the golden jubilee of profession of Fr. Adelhelm and the occasion where he was formally given the title and status of titular abbot, a recognition from Rome that acknowledged the role of Fr. Adelhelm in the founding and growth of Mount Angel Abbey. He was also made an honorary citizen of the city of Mt. Angel and given a key to the city. In his old age Fr. Adelhelm had taken on a venerable status that had eluded him in his earlier years. He could be counted on to keep alive the stories of the founding generation and maintain cordial relations with the multiple groups served by Mount Angel.

There are several indications of an improved status of the abbey's financial condition during the first five years of Abbot Placidus in office. The farm was expanding operations, showing improvement in its hop harvest and enlarging its dairy herd and chicken production,

16. *Abbey Chronicle* X (1913), 6.

Photo of titular abbot Adelhelm Odermatt on his golden jubilee celebration, September 29, 1916, with Bishop Schinner of Spokane and Madame Schumann-Heink.

while investing in mechanized equipment. Contracts were also signed to quarry stone from the abbey's mountain property. One other sign of financial confidence was the abbey's willingness to assume an outstanding debt of a nearby Trappist Abbey in Jordan, to the figure of $25,000. In exchange, the abbey was given jurisdiction of two parishes in Portland (Sacred Heart and St. Agatha) along with the parish in Mt. Angel and all of the county of Tillamook.[17]

17. Martinus Crawley, ed., *Monks of Jordan, 1904–2001* (Lafayette, OR: Guadalupe Translations, 2004) and *Abbey Chronicle* XI, 6. In 1904 six monks from the Trappist Abbey in Fontgombault, France came to Oregon, fleeing laic laws of the French government. They founded a monastery and it was dedicated by Archbishop Christie in 1907. With debts and a fire, it was decided in 1909 to bring the monks back to France. Some returned and others became priests of the archdiocese and a few monks of Mount Angel. The archdiocese took on the debt for a time and later agreed to let Mount Angel accept that responsibility in exchange for the parishes.

The Shadow of World War I

Perhaps the most trying and persistent of the challenges facing Abbot Placidus and the monastic community was the cloud of World War I. With entry of the United States into the conflict in 1917, a new series of tests visited the community. An anonymous letter arrived at the abbey in April of that year, shortly after the Declaration of War by Congress, accusing several monks of seditious speech. Incoming mail frequently bore the mark of "opened by the censor." Abbey schools ended their term in May rather than mid-June. Abbot Placidus was called to Portland in October of 1917 for an interview with the US District Attorney. He was informed that *St. Josephs Blatt,* like other German publications, now needed a license to publish. Clearly the community faced an unexpected and unprecedented series of challenges that put into question its patriotism and reputation.

In 1918 things took a turn for the worse. On April 4 orders from Washington, DC, suspended publication of both *St. Josephs Blatt* and *Armen Seelen Freund.* In September all of the monks between the ages of 31 and 46 were required to register for military service.[18] On September 19 a Department of Justice agent insisted on searching the rooms of Brother Michael Dunn and Frater Alcuin Heibel on the third floor of the abbey, following up on a suspicion lodged by a local resident who thought lights in these rooms in the pre-dawn hours were possible signaling codes.[19]

Even if there were some monks in the monastery who would not have favored American entry into the war, there were definite efforts to show allegiance to the United States. Father Adelhelm urged German-speaking Americans of the area to be faithful to the oath they had taken as citizens of the United States.[20] Father Idelphonse Calmus enlisted in the army as a chaplain and was sent to military duty at Camp Zachary Taylor in the fall of 1918. This set a standard of chaplains in the military

18. See "First World War," *Abbey Chronicle* XII, 6. Younger members of the community had been obliged to register a year earlier.

19. "First World War," 5.

20. Just before the war, in a letter to Abbot Frowin, Fr. Adelhelm complained of the American monks of Mount Angel not wanting to learn German, June 4, 1913, CAA.

service that was to continue for the Second World War, as well as the conflicts in Korea and Vietnam. In the climate of World War I, the service of Fr. Idelphonse was recognized by those outside the monastery as a sign of the patriotic convictions of the monks. In similar fashion, the move to discontinue serving wine and beer at table with the advent of prohibition became a way of exemplifying the Mount Angel community's patriotism and adherence to American rather than European customs.

The most acute threat to the community in the concluding weeks of the war in the fall of 1918 was the flu pandemic that swept the West Coast. Father Idelphonse became critically ill after ministering to the needs of seriously ill soldiers in his camp. On October 14, classes were suspended in the schools of Mount Angel. Student flu victims were placed in the seminary wing of the schools. Only two or three of the students became fatalities of the pandemic, and the monastic community, despite a number of cases, survived without a fatality. However, the ranks in the monastic choir were severely depleted during the weeks of October and early November, and the fear of the flu contagion that fall lingered for weeks on the hilltop.

A Return to Normalcy and a Resignation

With the signing of the armistice on November 11, 1918, a semblance of normalcy returned to Mount Angel. Classes resumed in mid-February with assurance that the flu pandemic had run its course. The *St. Josephs Blatt* appeared again in print.[21] Even though it continued to offer a German-language source of news and religious commentary, it became clear that German language and culture had none of the privileged position they enjoyed prior to the war.

It was through the *Blatt* that Brother Celestine made appeals for help for the displaced and hungry of Europe. Father Alcuin Heibel and the Benedictine sisters in the abbey kitchen helped to pack and distribute boxes of food and provisions to many needy Europeans.[22] This was a

21. At this time the *Mt. Angel Magazine* went from a monthly to a weekly publication and expanded to a nationwide audience.

22. See *Mount Angel Letter* (April 1972), 4.

prefiguring of the much larger outpouring of charitable work that was to be headed by Fr. Alcuin at the end of World War II.

The year 1920 signaled the close of the founding era at Mount Angel with the death of Fr. Adelhelm Odermatt on November 6. Still active almost up to the day of his death, he was the icon of Mount Angel's origins and a constant figure in its leadership for almost four decades. His passage from a man of controversy and constant activity to that of revered founder was yet another sign of communal maturity in the monastic community.

The year 1920 also marked the first retreat hosted by the abbey. Abbot Placidus had received a request from the Knights of Columbus to come to the hilltop. With abbatial assent, more than eighty men attended this first retreat and created a tradition that was continued by the abbots who came after him.

Even as Father Adelhelm was mourned, Abbot Placidus contemplated stepping down from his position. In a letter to Fr. Maurus Snyder in the summer of 1921, he wrote: "I become melancholy and morose and at times am absolutely unable to arouse myself to any initiative or action."[23] Abbot Placidus submitted his resignation on July 5, but it was only some time later that it was accepted in Rome.

Abbot Placidus deserves credit for steering the community through a troubled time in the aftermath of Abbot Thomas's resignation and of the turmoil of World War I. He set a precedent by refusing to keep the title of abbot and the insignia that were part of the office after he stepped down. Instead, he willingly served briefly in the Native American Mission in British Columbia, then as a pastor in Tillamook and Sacred Heart Parish in Portland, until failing health forced him to retire to the abbey. His quiet and prayerful presence in the community for almost two decades after his resignation was a fitting complement to his effective leadership during a difficult time.

An abbatial election was held on October 25, 1921, and it had significance for Mount Angel's history. It helped to lead Mount Angel into an era of native-born leadership and a period when new challenges confronted the community.

23. Letter of Abbot Placidus Fuerst to Fr. Maurus Snyder, August 28, 1921, MAAA.

Entering a New Era

Upon his election in October of
1921, Abbot Bernard Murphy carried the distinction of being the
first American-born superior of
Mount Angel.[24] He had been born
in Portland and his abbatial tenure coincided with the more rapid
assimilation of Mount Angel to
American ways. Prior to being
elected, Murphy had been director of Mount Angel Seminary for
three years (1903–6) and president of Mount Angel College for
two years (1908–10). From 1916 to
1921 he had served as subprior in
the community. The new superior
had traveled widely in Europe as a

Abbot Bernard Murphy, third abbot of
Mount Angel.

student and acquainted himself with Engelberg, Beuron, and a number
of other Benedictine monasteries on the continent. His familiarity
with the monastic practices and personages of Europe was to benefit
Mount Angel as it attempted to find a right balance between the best
usages of Europe and the necessary adaptation to American conditions. Abbot Bernard was another person whose monastic character
had been shaped by Abbot Frowin. As a student in Rome in 1898, he
initiated a correspondence with Conception's abbot. As noted earlier,
upon his return from Rome in late 1899, he stayed at Conception to
finish his dissertation and was impressed with the liturgy and the observance of the house. One of his reasons for choosing Conception was
the opportunity to have a prolonged period to be with Abbot Frowin.
In subsequent years, Fr. Bernard entrusted many of the concerns he
had about monastic life at Mount Angel to the wisdom and experience

24. Among other distinctions claimed by Abbot Bernard, he was the first native-
born American citizen and the first Oregonian to enter the community, as well as
the first native of Portland to be ordained to the priesthood.

of Abbot Frowin, particularly during the troubled time of the abbatial tenure of Abbot Thomas.

The new leadership team was completed with the naming of Abbot Bernard's old Roman classmate, Fr. Jerome Wespe, as prior and Fr. Thomas Meier as subprior. A year later, Fr. Thomas was also named as master of clerics and novices. An even more assertive sign of the transition into a more Americanized stage for Mount Angel was the declaration made by Abbot Bernard that no candidates for the abbey coming from German-speaking countries would be accepted into Mount Angel until they had spent at least two years in one of the abbey schools and had a facility with the English language.[25] The fact that Abbot Bernard had learned German during his days as a student in Europe and at Engelberg gave him greater credence in carrying out these directives. This new protocol spoke pointedly to the manner in which the assimilation process was now successfully being accomplished at Mount Angel.

Abbot Bernard felt an obligation to visit other monasteries and draw from them what was best liturgically and spiritually for Mount Angel. Accordingly, he went to Conception Abbey in June of 1922 for the blessing of its new abbot, Philip Ruggle. He wrote back to his confreres, giving a hint of his own fondest hopes for an eventual abbey church in Oregon: "Oh if only you could be here and hear the Divine Office in the great Abbey Church. Yesterday afternoon as I sat and listened to the glorious antiphons re-echoing through the church and saw the splendor of the Ceremonial, I hardly knew whether to weep or rejoice. It is simply wonderful, elevating one's soul above the sordid world. I hope and pray that we may soon have [at Mount Angel] a house worthy of God."[26] In that same year Abbot Bernard traveled to the Isle of Wight off of England to visit the Solesmes monks of Quarr Abbey, and he went on to spend time at Beuron, revisiting the abbey where he had first stayed as a student in 1897 and attesting to the high

---

25. "Abbot Bernard Sets a New Course," *Abbey Chronicle* XVI, 4. The last group of Europeans to enter the community were two young Swiss men who came back with Fr. Adelhelm after his trip to Switzerland in 1919.

26. Letter of Abbot Bernard Murphy to confreres, June 11, 1922, Conception, MO, MAAA.

standard of observance and liturgy he found once again.[27] Abbot Bernard included a visit to his old haunts in Rome at Sant'Anselmo, to Monte Cassino, to the Swiss abbeys of Engelberg and Einsiedeln, and the Bavarian monastery of St. Boniface in Munich—all places that were influences on Mount Angel's history. In the process of this Benedictine pilgrimage, ideas of monastic observance and the nature of an abbey church were developed that would be put into practice back in Oregon.

Given the geographic isolation of Mount Angel from so many of the Benedictine communities in the Midwest and mid-Atlantic states, it was all the more important for Abbot Bernard to acquaint the hilltop community with the liturgical and spiritual channels of thought and practice that were taking place at this time in Europe. A residual outcome of this effort was the continuance of the policy of monks sent to Europe for studies, so that they could imbibe some of the same richness.

A Changing Face of Community

The early 1920s coincided with the initiative on the part of the schools to receive accreditation through the channel of local educational agencies. The college was reorganized and was accredited by the Northwest Association of Secondary and Higher Schools in 1925. Father Alcuin Heibel was named dean of the college in 1922 and began a long career of spearheading higher education on the hilltop by visiting other colleges and universities in the summer of that year and incorporating the best practices of these institutions for Mount Angel. Father Benedict Barr was made rector of the seminary and began its updating in 1921. This represented a new effort on the part of the educational mission of Mount Angel to adapt to the categories of professionalism in American education and to forge an identity as a respectable institution of higher education for its college and seminary.

Mount Angel, along with many Catholic institutions, faced a new tide of anti-Catholic sentiment in the years after World War I. The passage of prohibition laws both locally and nationally was seen by some as a reaction to practices by many Catholics of alcohol use that had been carried from their country of origin. A resurgent Ku Klux Klan

27. Letter of Abbot Bernard Murphy to confreres at Mount Angel, *Mt. Angel Magazine* 24, no. 18 (March 2, 1923), 12.

Fr. Alcuin Heibel at his desk in the college.

was powerful in Oregon and in many other states, with a new focus on opposition to Jews and Catholics, as well as African Americans. Legislative efforts were put in place, both on the state and federal level, to curb immigration from countries of Catholic origin and to restrict the freedom of Catholic schools.

All of the above were issues taken up by the print apostolate of Mount Angel. The *Mt. Angel Magazine* now carried a revealing sub-head: *A Catholic National Weekly of America.* One can scan the weekly pages of this publication in the postwar years and find detailed and acute commentary on much of this anti-Catholic sentiment. The magazine was one of the first printed sources to criticize the Oregon Compulsory Public School Education Act of 1922, which effectively made public schools the only option for all Oregonians.[28] The fact that this act was struck down by the Oregon Supreme Court in 1924 and by the US Supreme Court three years later (in *Pierce v. Society of Sisters)* was welcomed as a just vindication of inherently discriminatory laws.

In a similar way, the *Magazine* and the Benedictines of Oregon pointed out the evils of the Ku Klux Klan as a negative force in American public life. Already in the previous decade, there was a salacious example

28. *Mt. Angel Magazine* (November 27, 1922), 9. The *Magazine* also spoke against the "Garb Bill" in the following year that prevented Catholic sisters from entering a public school in religious dress (February 9, 1923).

of Klan-like religious prejudice in a nativist pamphlet that purportedly described the nefarious escape from Our Lady of the Angels Convent in Mt. Angel by a woman (with Klan contacts) who recounted a standard litany of anti-Catholic prejudice.[29] The shadow of the Klan was a palpable menace for many Catholic families that lived in the regions around Mount Angel. Monks who had entered the monastery in the 1930s and 1940s from these areas retained vivid accounts of how their physical safety and freedom to practice their faith were compromised by acts of open hostility from Klan members.

Another instance of Mount Angel publications confronting what was judged as prejudice against Catholics came from south of the US border. There was a steady skein of editorial criticisms leveled against the Calles regime in Mexico on account of the anti-Catholic policies initiated there in the 1920s. This was an instance of how the Press at Mount Angel widened the horizons of their readership, for few Catholics in North America at the time were aware of the brutality of the anti-Catholic policies of the anti-clerical Mexican government or the *Cristero* revolt against it. This was a particularly telling critique in light of the subsequent ventures undertaken in Mexico by Mount Angel monks Fr. Alcuin Heibel and Fr. Ambrose Zenner.

There was a notable change in the 1920s with an Irish-American abbot and a student body and monastic community that had fewer old-world features attached to it. The increased emphasis given to athletic competition in the college and an observable increase in patriotic practices and symbols were additional markers of a transition to a more assimilated and confident hilltop community. Technology also made its appearances in these years. Father Benedict Barr installed phones throughout the abbey and radios became prominent for the students and the monks.

Enrollment in the schools showed a marked upswing. The farm operation and the Press were both proud of their modernization and profitability. The continued increase in membership of the abbey and

---

29. J. E. Hosmer, *The Escaped Nun from Mt. Angel Convent* (Silverton, OR: Silverton Journal, 1913). This scurrilous tract was in imitation of some of the infamous nativist tracts of an earlier era in American history—and was without any truthful foundation.

A baseball game on the sports field in May of 1926. Visible on the far
right is the garage where the fire of September 20–21, 1926, originated.

the expanding pastoral obligations in nearby parishes underlined
the mood of optimism that was a mirror of the uplift felt by many
American Catholics in the early 1920s.

A Presence Among Native Americans

One of the earliest pastoral commitments of Mount Angel was to missionary work with the Native American people of the Northwest. In
1899, at the request of Archbishop Alexander Christie, the monks of
Mount Angel were invited to accept two missions on the West Coast
of Vancouver Island in British Columbia. At a community meeting
in that same year the monastery decided to send three of its priest
monks to investigate the site. Upon their return the invitation from
the Archbishop was accepted.[30] In May of 1900, Frs. Maurus Snyder
and Charles Moser left for Vancouver Island. There they joined a group
of Benedictine sisters from Queen of Angels Convent at Clayoquot to

30. *Abbey Chronicle* V, 6.

Fr. Charles Moser on his way to the
Christie School in Vancouver Island, BC.

establish a school and a mission. Throughout the next few decades there was a steady presence of Mount Angel monks in Vancouver and at Native American missions. Father Charles was to stay on Vancouver Island for over a quarter of a century at the mission of Kaskawis and what became known as the Christie school. In all, fourteen monks from Mount Angel lived in the missions on Vancouver Island between 1900 and 1938.[31]

While it is not easy to assess the pastoral effectiveness of the community's missionary efforts with the Native Americans, it is helpful to know that Mount Angel was not alone among American Benedictines in accepting this work. At the same time as the first monks were leaving for Vancouver Island, monks of Conception and St. Meinrad Abbeys were actively engaged in missionary work on the Northern Plains. The American-Cassinese Congregation monks were also committed to providing education and pastoral assistance for Native Americans on several reservations in northern Minnesota, while the Benedictine Sisters of Queen of Angels Convent were even more widespread in their work among the Native Americans of the Northwest than the monks of Mount Angel.[32] The missionary methods may have fallen short of the preferred inculturation of later years, but the stable Benedictine presence won the confidence of local Native American

31. Andreas Eckerstorfer, OSB, "To Do Some Good Among the Indians: Mount Angel Benedictines as Missionaries on the West Coast of Vancouver Island," a paper written for the theology department of Mount Angel Seminary, 1994.

32. From the 1880s, the sisters were asked to minister to the Native American reservation at Grand Ronde. Alberta Dieker, OSB, "Rooted in Faith: The Early History of the Benedictine Sisters of Mt. Angel, Oregon," *American Benedictine Review* 58, no. 4 (December 2007), 375.

Fr. Maurus Snyder in top row and Benedictine sisters with students of the Christie School.

tribes and quality education was provided to indigenous children that otherwise would not have been available.

The Passing of Two Pillars

The first years of Abbot Bernard's tenure coincided with the passing from the scene of two people who played instrumental roles in Mount Angel's development.

Abbot Frowin Conrad died at Conception Abbey on March 24, 1923. A catalogue of his contributions to Mount Angel requires much space. What became increasingly evident to the first generation of Mount Angel monks was that without the sure guidance and example of Abbot Frowin, especially in the period from 1899 to 1915, the Oregon community might easily have floundered. His allegiance to Mount Angel grew with the years, and the significant sacrifice of time and labor he made to ensure the monastic vitality and stability of the monastery will remain as a treasured legacy in Mount Angel's history.

On April 6, 1925, Archbishop Alexander Christie died in Portland. He had been archbishop for over a quarter century and in that time when Mount Angel faced many challenges, he had given unstinting support to its efforts. He gladly came to the monastery for the blessing of abbots, ordinations of young monks, and the general support of the abbey's mission. In much the same way as Archbishop Gross ingratiated himself to the monastery by giving retreats to the community and spending time in knowing the monks, Archbishop Christie made himself accessible to the community, while allowing it a free hand to run its schools and carry on its pastoral and sacramental work. At a time when some bishops did not share a congenial relationship with religious communities in their diocese, Archbishop Christie set an example of firm support for both the pastoral and monastic character of Mount Angel's mission, an example that his successors would follow.

The Fire and Aftermath

The circumstances of the fire on the night of September 20–21, 1926, are worth noting. September 20 was registration day for all three of the schools. Returning students came with their personal belongings and prepared for a deserved night's sleep. Instead, many were awoken around midnight by cries from their prefects of a fire that was spreading and would require a rapid evacuation, but only after student-organized efforts were made to save articles from the chapel, library, and gymnasium. The fire had cut off power for the water supply in the abbey water tank. The nearby fire departments could do little but try and manage the fire that had spread to most of the hilltop. By the time at first light when the fire had burned itself out, only the Post Office and Benedictine Press were found to be spared among all the buildings on the hilltop.

Personal accounts of the fire and its source are legion. The most likely source of the fire was an open garage door located close to both the monastery and seminary buildings. Sometime between 11:00 and 11:30 p.m. on the night of September 20, a pickup truck with bags of drying abbey hops returned to the garage. The particular cause of the fire remains in dispute. Some thought a spark from the truck or a tossed cigarette may have been the agent. Others believe a barrel of stored oil rags in the corner of the garage, noted by a fire inspector in the days before the fire, could have been the cause. What is beyond dispute is that the fire spread rapidly from its source and soon engulfed surrounding buildings.

The monastery before the fire of 1926.

The monastery ruins after the 1926 fire.

As is often the case in such disasters, there was a mixture of heroism and chaos at work on the hilltop that night. Father Alcuin Heibel, then the rector of the college, deserves credit for calling first the Mt. Angel Fire Department and then the Salem Department. In the latter case, the Salem firemen were able to bring water to cover the Press and Post Office and prevent the embers of the fire from affecting these two edifices that stood on the far side of the hill. Father Alcuin also ordered the students to pack their effects that many of them had carried in only that day and leave the college wing.[33] Father Maurus helped to direct people into cars that brought them down the hilltop to the St. Mary's school and parish hall. Under the leadership of St. Mary's pastor, Fr. Dominic Weadenschwyler, the members of the parish made hasty provision for the housing and care of students and monks, many of whom were still

33. This was after the students had helped to remove from the chapel all of the religious objects, books, and even the pews. See Martin Pollard's "Eyewitness Account" in *Abbey Chronicle* XXI, 4–6.

in a daze. The power outage and lack of electricity only exacerbated the fear and disorientation of the inhabitants on the hilltop. The older monks, in particular, found the night to be a traumatizing ordeal.

In terms of the buildings affected by the fire, the entire complex of monastery, school, and outlying buildings was in ruins. Some of the material loss was hard to calculate. The Abbey Library, for example, had over 20,000 volumes, along with incunabula and manuscripts from the sixteenth century. Among those books and rare documents that were pushed out of windows in a desperate effort to save them, only a few were not ruined in the water and debris. The abbey's museum collection was also a total loss.[34]

The chapel was the first area where people rushed to take out the Blessed Sacrament, vessels of the altar, vestments, statues, and choir books. Even the pews were removed.[35] The efforts of students were heroic as they removed from the buildings what they could before the structures were engulfed in flame.

With respect to dollar calculation, the loss was estimated at more than one million dollars. The mortgaged buildings were insured at only 10 percent of their replacement value.[36] Many of the students had lost all of their personal cash and checks that were still in their travel luggage, and untold personal effects of the monks and students were never recovered.

The monks gathered the morning of September 21 at the base of the hill in the parish church, rectory, and school of St. Mary's Parish. One positive realization was that no lives were lost, and there were no serious injuries. The monastic community was willing to give thanks for that and their first common action after the disaster was to pray the Divine Office (choir books had been saved) and offer Mass in the parish church. That day, Fr. Dominic, along with the parishioners and townspeople of Mt. Angel, opened their homes and their hearts to the monastery and student body. Makeshift classrooms were created so that classes could resume for the day students and seminarians. Space

---

34. McCrank, *Mt. Angel Abbey*, 100.
35. *Abbey Chronicle* XXI, 4.
36. McCrank, *Mt. Angel Abbey*, 65.

was found to accommodate all the members of the monastic community, then over seventy in number.

The shock and the scope of the loss became evident in the days after the fire. The most immediate concerns facing the community were how to go about rebuilding and how to find the financial resources to do so. Abbot Bernard, on the night of the fire, had been found in the abbey cemetery (where the Blessed Sacrament had been taken into the chapel there). Traumatized by the flames that destroyed his community's buildings, he took up temporary residence in the chaplain's quarters of the Benedictine sisters. He called for a meeting of the chapter of the abbey on October 26. Both Abbot Bernard and his prior, Fr. Jerome Wespe, had experienced the first fire of 1892, and knew firsthand of the arduous challenge faced by the community in that earlier time. Records of the chapter meeting show that Abbot Bernard exhorted the community to make a decision to build as soon as possible. His words to the community at that meeting convey eloquently the crucial step the abbey faced:

> We must decide the question of building anew the abbey and whatever was destroyed by the fire. Matters have reached such a pass that we must think of erecting a new monastery as soon as possible if our community is to continue its existence. As I remarked on the day of the fire: this fire will be a blessing or a curse for the community of Mount Angel Abbey.[37]

Abbot Bernard's address to the chapter emphasized the gravity of the moment and the precariousness of the community's position, but it also tapped into a deep vein of self-sacrifice and resourcefulness that was at the core of the community. It appeared to have the desired effect, for the result was that a majority of the abbey chapter members voted to rebuild. That was rendered more precise in subsequent chapter meetings of November 8 and December 30, when the monks reaffirmed their conviction to build on the hilltop and to accept the plan for the new buildings that had been proposed by Fr. Sebastian Terhaar.[38]

37. From chapter minutes of October 26, 1926, MAAA.
38. See chapter minutes of November 8 and December 30, 1926, MAAA.

Appealing for Funds and Rebuilding

Developments in the first weeks after the disaster took on significance. Thanks to the preservation of the Press, the *Mt. Angel Magazine* and the *St. Josephs Blatt* issued urgent appeals to its readers throughout the country. At this juncture the role of the Press in the life of the community should be highlighted. The Benedictine Press was tightly associated with the community from 1889, with the first issue of *St. Josephs Blatt.* The original Press building was destroyed in the first fire of 1892. By 1908 it had joined the monastery at the top of the hill under the management of Br. Celestine Mueller, who was to maintain that position until his death in 1929. Brother Celestine promoted state-of-the-art technology with an eye to Benedictine frugality. An example of the latter is the acquisition after the San Francisco earthquake of 1906 of a web press from the *San Francisco Examiner* newspaper. A number of Benedictine sisters from the Queen of Angels community assisted Br. Celestine in proofreading and typesetting in the first few decades before the 1926 fire. The Press also benefited from the establishment of the Saint Benedict Post Office in July of 1914. Having the Press adjacent to the Post Office expedited the mailings sent out, including the *Mt. Angel Magazine.* It was the regular fundraising appeals that appeared in the *Magazine,* along with firsthand accounts of the ravages of the fire, that moved many to make their contributions to the abbey.

Recognizing the priority of securing financial aid, a central office for soliciting funds was established at St. Joseph's Hall next to the parish. In imitation of what Fr. Adelhelm had done after the first fire, a number of monks were sent out to raise funds for the rebuilding. Fathers Alcuin, Gabriel Morrisroe, and Michael Reilly were entrusted with this work.[39] The community was also helped immeasurably by a return visit of the Abbot Primate, Fidelis von Stotzingen. The primate had enjoyed the hospitality of the Mount Angel community during a visit at the end of August in 1926. He was in Idaho when news of the fire reached him, and he returned to Mount Angel in the days after

---

39. Neil Yocum, OSB, ed., *Mount of Communion: Mount Angel Abbey 1882–1982* (Salem, OR: Capital City Graphics, 1985), 32. Father Alcuin remained the monk who did this work for the longest time and with the most fruitful results.

1927 aerial photo of ruins of the monastery, with the Press Building on the lower right and rebuilt monastery on the far left of the monastery.

the fire, when he encouraged the monks to rebuild and pledged the assistance of the wider Benedictine world. In tandem with Europe, a number of Benedictine monasteries throughout the country came to the aid of Mount Angel.[40] This was another instance of how contacts in Europe and elsewhere in the monastic world were to accrue to benefits for the Mount Angel community. The recently blessed archbishop of Portland, Edward Howard,[41] initiated a campaign of financial help through the archdiocese, beginning with a special collection taken up in all the parishes of the archdiocese on Sunday, October 3.

40. *Mt. Angel Magazine*, October issues. A sign of the interest and support of Mount Angel by the abbeys of the Swiss-American Congregation was their decision to hold their General Chapter at the new monastery in April of 1929.

41. Archbishop Edward Howard was named the fifth archbishop of Oregon City on April 30, 1926. On September 26, just days after the Mount Angel fire, the Archdiocesan See was officially named as Portland. Archbishop Howard was to serve as the Ordinary for Portland and for the monastic community for an unprecedented forty years and was a frequent visitor to the hilltop.

Photo of monastery with walkway in 1928.

Perhaps more surprising was the response of some of the non-Catholic institutions of Oregon to the plight of the monastic community. The *Oregon Daily Press*, the *Oregon Daily Journal*, the Portland *Oregonian*, and the Salem *Capital Journal* all issued calls of assistance for the monks of Mount Angel.[42] The generous response of civic community leaders constituted a sign of just how high in esteem the community had become in their regard. The alleviation of some of the strong nativist currents in the aftermath of the fire was one of the few observable positive fruits that came from the tragedy.

The time period after the fire saw the monks continue their regular round of observance and classes in the schools. This newly adjusted regularity brought about yet another fruit of the fire's aftermath— a closer connection between the townspeople of Mt. Angel and the monastery. The people had literally opened their doors to the monks and students at this critical time, and there seemed to be an unspoken pledge that the citizenry of the town and most particularly the people of St. Mary's Parish were committed to helping the monastic community get back on its feet.

At the urging of Fr. Dominic, who had been the first rector of the seminary, the classes in the seminary were the first ones to recom-

42. McCrank, *Mt. Angel Abbey*, 65.

Abbot Bernard presiding at the laying of the cornerstone for the new monastery, July 17, 1927.

mence. Less than two weeks after the fire, to the amazement of all, the seminary was in session in makeshift classrooms. The college students were not asked to come back until the next academic year.

By the spring of 1927, the site of the former monastery and school buildings on the hilltop had been cleared of the debris from the fire. Landscaping began, and Fr. Sebastian, whose comprehensive plan for Mount Angel had been approved by the monastic chapter, worked in cooperation with the Portland architectural firm of Barrett and Logan to begin construction of the new abbey and church.[43] At the same time, the community was given permission by Rome to borrow up to $125,000 for the construction effort. On July 17, 1927, the cornerstone for the new abbey was laid with Abbot Bernard present, along with a crowd that was estimated at 2,500 people. Despite delays due to weather and materials, the monks were ready by the next year to relocate. On the Feast of St. Joseph, March 19, 1928, the monastic community prayed the Divine Office for the last time in the parish

43. "The Tremendous Task of Rebuilding," *Abbey Chronicle* XXII, 4. A leader of the architectural firm was an alumnus of the school, Robert Barrett.

church of St. Mary's and then marched in procession up to the new abbey chapel and monastery. They celebrated Mass, led by Prior Jerome Wespe, settled in their new quarters, and had their first common meal on the hilltop since September 20, 1926. Two days later, Archbishop Howard blessed the monastic church, still under construction but able to be used for worship. The south part of the abbey building was temporarily used by the resident seminarians and day students for their classes. The junior monks, in particular, were much involved in the daunting job of planting and landscaping of the site. Two white marble statues—of the Guardian Angel and the Sacred Heart—that survived the fire were put in place on either side of the church and remain there today.

Notwithstanding the optimistic mood generated by the relocation and new building, the monks felt keenly the burden of the rebuilding enterprise. A representative account of that attitude was registered in a letter sent back to Engelberg by Br. Michael Dunn: "On St. Joseph's Feast we all moved up to the new abbey and on St. Benedict's Feast we had a great celebration with the Archbishop singing Pontifical Mass. . . . The Abbey grounds are badly in need of improvement, but nothing is done as we have no money left. Perhaps you could find some in Europe."[44]

Hindsight permits one to see that the community was fortunate that the fire was followed by three years of a strong economy that allowed for the collection of funds and favorable conditions for interest on loans. With the stock market crash in the fall of 1929 and the ensuing period of the Great Depression, the circumstances of rebuilding and funding were rendered more problematic. An arresting fact is how the monks during this time were reluctant to sell any of their extensive land holdings as a means of lessening the crisis, another manifestation of Benedictine stewardship, as was the beautification of the hilltop that took shape in the decades following 1926.

The years after the fire took their toll, emotionally and physically, on the monastic community. Seven monks died in the three-year period after the fire, including Br. Celestine, the editor of the *St. Josephs Blatt*. Abbot Bernard continued to be plagued by difficulty with his vision. His

---

44. Letter of Br. Michael Dunn to Fr. Maurus of Engelberg, May 17, 1928, MAAA.

Photo of finished Aquinas Hall in 1932.

time away from the monastery, for reasons of both health and business, was another cross for the community to bear. But there were examples of endurance and sacrifice as well. Brother Gabriel Loerch, one of the lay brother carpenters, was requested by Abbot Bernard to fashion a set of black walnut hand-carved choir stalls for the church. This he did,

finishing just prior to his death in January of 1932. Father Norbert Matteucci, having labored to build the new abbey edifice in 1927–28, oversaw the construction of the new student residence, Aquinas Hall. This new facility was partially completed in 1930 and was able to welcome students in the fall of that year. Throughout this period of determined work and sacrifice, the abbey continued to send monks to Europe for further education, another expression of confidence in the future.

When one considers the shock of the second fire of 1926 and the critical state of the Mount Angel

Photo of Br. Gabriel Loerch, abbey carpenter and craftsman of church pews, by the old monastery goldfish pond.

community's financial health and social morale in its aftermath, a wider historical context is of help. There are examples of other American Benedictine monasteries of men in the decade of the 1920s that had to declare bankruptcy and, because of natural disasters and the start of the Great Depression, suffered greatly. Assumption Abbey in North Dakota and Sacred Heart Monastery in Oklahoma are two of the more prominent examples. Given the relative physical isolation of Mount Angel and its presence in the midst of a state and region that was not receptive to Catholic institutions, early wagers on Mount Angel's ability to bounce back from the losses suffered in the fire might have seemed freighted with doubts. But the community's resilience and determination became evident in monks and students, neighbors and faraway monastic confreres. The positive response to Mount Angel rising from the ashes was one that signaled the broad mantle of support the monks were blessed to share.

CHAPTER FOUR

Recovery and Growth

Another Leadership Transition

THE HEALTH OF ABBOT BERNARD took a turn for the worse in 1933. An operation to correct his failing eyesight in New York City was not successful. The abbot was legally blind, and his ability to lead the community effectively was curtailed. He was fortunate to have as his second-in-command Prior Fr. Jerome Wespe. Father Jerome was a steady and saintly presence, respected by all in the community. He was another of the stalwart monks of the founding generation who became an icon of stability and monastic observance.

Father Jerome deserves a privileged place in the select circle of indispensable people for Mount Angel's growth in the first half of the twentieth century. His twin roles of prior and master of ceremonies for the period between the wars were invaluable gifts to the community. As prior, he was the epitome of duty, finding a way to maintain order and decorum even in the trying months after the fire of 1926. As master of ceremonies, he kept contact with European centers of monastic life, especially his beloved Beuron. He adapted much of their liturgical and monastic ritual to Mount Angel and insured that it would be accomplished with reverence and regard for tradition. It was a tradition he passed on to his successor as master of ceremonies, Fr. Robert Keber, who had been immersed in the monasticism of Beuron through his studies at the *Academia Benedictina* in Maria Laach. It seemed fitting for someone who had internalized much of the important events of Mount Angel's history that in the last year of his life Fr. Jerome served

Fr. Jerome Wespe cutting wood.

as official archivist for the community, safeguarding the story he had lived so intensely.

Overriding his sense of duty, there were few monks who could match the reputation for sanctity that Fr. Jerome demonstrated by his way of life. From the lay brothers he served at the Milk Ranch in his early years as a priest to the long lines of confreres who would claim him as their confessor in the years after he served as prior, Fr. Jerome left a template of holiness of life and single-mindedness of monastic commitment. He truly became a backbone for the community's recovery after the fire.

With the counsel of his canonical adviser, Fr. Augustine Bachofen, and at the prompting of Abbot Philip Ruggle, abbot president of the Swiss-American Congregation, Abbot Bernard submitted a request for an abbot coadjutor to succeed him in exercising legitimate authority and governance of the monastery. The petition of Abbot Bernard was granted and on August 1, 1934, an election was held.

Given the dominant role Fr. Jerome played as prior in managing abbey affairs during the extended periods of Abbot Bernard's absence and his long and distinguished service to the community, many thought he would be the natural choice of the community as the next abbot. However, as the monks gathered for the election, Fr. Jerome deliv-

The community on the day of the election of Abbot Thomas Meier, August 1, 1934.

ered an unambiguous statement that he was not a candidate and would not accept the position if elected.[1]

It was no surprise that the chapter then turned to the subprior and novice master, Fr. Thomas Meier, as the fourth abbot of Mount Angel. Abbot Thomas was raised in Salem, Oregon, and received his education from the high school at Mount Angel. Like his predecessors, Abbot Thomas served the community in a variety of ways. He had been a prefect in the college for three years, and for two years was head of the college. He served as master of clerics and novices for a number of years until the time of his election. Abbot Thomas was given charge of a community of eighty-two monks. It was a mix of forty-five priest-monks, twenty-four lay brothers, eleven monks in various years of formation before solemn profession, and two claustral oblates who lived in the monastery with a promise of obedience to the abbot. The stage was set for Abbot Thomas to institute a number of changes in the life of the community.

A priority in order of change was to be in the liturgy of the monastery. One of the first appointments made by Abbot Thomas was for

---

1. *Abbey Chronicle* XXIX (1934), 6. Father Jerome was given a well-deserved vacation in Europe by Abbot Thomas after the election, only to come back again as prior upon his return.

Fr. Victor Rassier to go to the Abbey of Solesmes in France for a year of intense study of Gregorian chant. This was to be in preparation for the decision of Abbot Thomas to implement the French Solesmes chant at Mount Angel, a change from the German chant they had used previously. Abbot Bernard and Fr. Jerome Wespe had already promoted a return to some of the choral and liturgical practices of Beuron and Solesmes, and Abbot Thomas continued in this vein. Accompanying this change was a restoration of sung vespers in July of 1936. This was ordered by Abbot Thomas to be in accord with the practice that had been in place in the earliest years of the abbey and to enhance the dignity of the Divine Office. Father Victor, as choirmaster, instructed the community in the use of their new choir books and set up regular practices for the schola and the monastic choir. A more intricate protocol of choir etiquette was also established.[2] Another way of underlining the dignity of the liturgy was to have all professions of vows take place at the daily High Mass rather than the Communion Mass in the early morning.

In subsequent years under Abbot Thomas there was an installation of a pipe organ (1938), and more formal training was given to the monks for liturgical practices. These liturgical changes were in part precipitated by a visit that then-Fr. Thomas Meier had made in 1928 to abbeys of Europe, a period when the Liturgical Movement was well underway. In many ways, this was a reprise of the model Abbot Bernard had left, consciously distilling through personal integration the liturgical and aesthetic bounty of European monasteries. The initiatives of Abbot Thomas were endorsed too by several of the Mount Angel monks, such as Fr. Martin Pollard and Fr. Luke Eberle, who had been exposed to the Liturgical Movement firsthand during their stay in European abbeys such as Maria Laach while studying in Europe. It ensured that Mount Angel would have a window to new liturgical developments well before other communities on the West Coast. Perhaps the best example of this was seen in the introduction of the *Missa Recitata* in early 1938 for the seminarians and the laity.[3] This was the form of the Mass, using St. Andrew Missals with parallel texts in Latin and English, that encouraged the congregation to respond to the prayers from the priest. Supported by Archbishop Howard and

---

2. "Highlights of 1936," *Abbey Chronicle* XXXII, 5.
3. *Abbey Chronicle* XXXIV, 5.

Photo of Abbot Thomas
Meier and Archduke Otto von
Hapsburg, October 13, 1949.

guided by some of the monks of Mount Angel who had taken part
in this liturgy at Maria Laach in the 1920s, it offered one of the first
models of active participation of the congregation in the liturgy, long
before the liturgical reforms of the Second Vatican Council.

Abbot Thomas, when he served as novice master under Abbot Bernard, was responsible for the training of candidates for the clerical
monks—those who would be going on for priestly ordination—and
for lay brothers. In this he paid particular attention to the condition
of the lay brothers. For example, the brothers had a separate chapel
for their prayers, along with a separate recreation room. In the refectory, the place of the brothers was in the middle of the dining room,
at tables covered with an oilcloth (unlike the linen at the other tables)
and with knives and forks with wooden handles, unlike the silverware
of the rest of the community.[4] This was not unlike conditions in other
Benedictine houses in the United States at the time. At Mount Angel,

4. From oral recollections of Fr. Thomas Brockhaus, Mount Angel Abbey Archives (hereafter MAAA).

Abbot Thomas recognized an ongoing challenge. On the one hand, he had to meet the needs of the remaining German-speaking brothers, who were content to pray separately from the community and practice their crafts and the maintenance of the monastery. On the other hand, he saw the need to take account of the new American vocations among the brothers who wanted more inclusion into the community life. In an effort to respond to the wishes of the American-born lay brothers, Abbot Thomas proposed that all of the prayers in the Brothers' Chapel would henceforth be in English. The change seems to have produced its desired effect, with the German-speaking brothers joining their younger confreres.[5] As part of this change, Abbot Thomas proposed to the chapter that they allow the lay brothers to occupy places in the choir stalls during Divine Office and the daily High Mass. While the community agreed that the brothers should be seen as part of the community, they felt that the distinction of separation should remain.[6]

Nonetheless, Abbot Thomas found ways to bring about a greater incorporation of the lay brothers into the mainstream of community life. He recalled Fr. Francis Burger from Christie Industrial School and appointed him as new director of the formation of the lay brothers. He requested that Fr. Augustine Bachofen be a regular preacher and lecturer for the lay brothers.[7] This latter move gave greater legitimacy to an equal spiritual formation for both prospective priest-monks and brothers. Another means of encouraging greater adaptation for the brothers was the decision of Abbot Thomas to send brothers to St. Meinrad in the 1940s to study and learn of the new methods of instructing American-born brothers that had been organized there by Abbot Ignatius Esser. This was in tandem with a summer trip by Fr. Clement Frank, the master of brothers, to visit several abbeys for the purpose of studying the different methods of training lay brothers.[8] All of these efforts served as one more sign of the Americanization or assimilation process that took place at Mount Angel in the two decades after World War I.

Mention should be made of the role played by Fr. Augustine Bachofen as a visiting monk during much of Abbot Thomas's tenure.

5. *Abbey Chronicle* XXX, 6.

6. Chapter minutes of November 30, 1939.

7. Diary entry of Fr. Augustine Bachofen, Archives of Conception Abbey (hereafter CAA).

8. *Abbey Chronicle* XXXVIII (1942), 6.

Br. Fidelis Schoenberger feeding chickens.

Fr. Augustine was a European-born and educated monk of Conception Abbey. He was a renowned canon lawyer who published the first English commentary on the *Code of Canon Law* that was issued in 1917. It ran to eight volumes and was published between 1918 and 1922. One constant in the long arc of Fr. Augustine's monastic life was his opposition to the Beuronese influence in the Benedictine Order, and this may have been a principal reason why he decided to leave Conception and go to Mount Angel in 1926. He was present at the time of the fire, and one of his rare open compliments given to the community as a whole was the manner in which he described them becoming more unified in the months and years after the fire. Even though he was a professed monk of Conception Abbey, he remained at Mount Angel until his death in December of 1943, when he was buried in the abbey cemetery. He taught in the seminary and served as a canonical consultant for Abbot Bernard. He kept a diary that provides keen insight and unsparing critiques on the life and times of Mount Angel in the seventeen years of his stay there.

Some of the criticisms leveled by Fr. Augustine were pointed and important for superiors to hear. For example, he chided those who had the fraters teaching in the college even as they were enrolled as students in the seminary.[9] He rightly noted that it went against canon

9. Diary entry of January 5, 1931, CAA.

law and placed both a physical and psychological burden on the fraters. In a similar critique, he did not think it prudent to ordain monks after their third year of theological studies, arguing that they should complete their full program of study first. There was an anti-authoritarian streak in Fr. Augustine's life. His relationship with abbots at Conception Abbey and Mount Angel was a tense one. Much of that can be attributed to his sardonic take on superiors, a sentiment found in a diary entry of 1936: "Most of our abbots—not all—are barking dogs at General Chapters and Culpa Chapters and know damned little about the psychology of the men they have to deal with. And we have to tolerate them forever!"[10] Yet this coarse critic of abbots was mindful of the latitude he was given at Mount Angel by Abbot Bernard and Abbot Thomas and knew that he was "tolerated" far more than he expected to be.

Father Augustine is representative of another strain of the life at Mount Angel. He was manifestly an intellectual, well-read, and admired for his experiences of travel and interaction with church leadership. The fact that he felt comfortable in writing sometimes biting commentary in his diary and was uncensored in his classroom teaching and while preaching in parishes says a great deal about Mount Angel's adaptive capacity for individual characters. No less it underscores the fact that monk-scholars found Mount Angel a receptive place to continue their work at a time when the life of those pursuing intellectual efforts was not often given primacy of place in religious orders.

New Ventures in British Columbia and Changes in the Schools

In 1938 Abbot Thomas announced that the long established Native American missions on Vancouver Island in British Columbia would be handed over to the Oblates of Mary Immaculate. This represented the close of a long and dedicated presence of Mount Angel monks at these missions. As has already been noted, the Mount Angel chapter had voted in 1899 to attend to these missions, and many monks had devoted the better part of their lives to serving the needs of the native population. They had shared in this with Benedictine women of Queen

10. Diary entry of January 19, 1936, CAA.

Blessing of the foundation cross and the founding monks by Abbot Thomas Meier on occasion of their departure for Mission, BC, September 14, 1939.

of Angels Convent, especially in conducting the Christie Residential School. The investment made by both communities of men and women to the work among the Kakawi Native Americans at Clayoquat was of ample portion and deeply appreciated by the indigenous population. As a sign of gratitude, place names on the western coast of Vancouver Island honored some of the missionary monks of Vancouver Island: Moser Point and Fr. Charles Channel for Fr. Charles Moser; Epper Passage for Fr. Frowin Epper; Rassier Point for Fr. Victor Rassier; Maurus Channel for Fr. Maurus Snyder; and Schindler Point for Fr. Joseph Schindler.[11]

At the same time as monks were leaving the Native American missions on Vancouver Island, Abbot Thomas encouraged the community to respond to the invitation of the Archbishop of Vancouver, British Columbia, to have monks of Mount Angel manage his minor seminary and make a monastic foundation. Taking on such an enterprise while Mount Angel was still in a recovery mode from its fire and

11. See *Mount Angel Letter* (March 1954), 3.

the vicissitudes of the Great Depression was no small matter. Abbot Thomas, in the summer of 1939, urged his community to make a choice on this request from British Columbia and called a series of community meetings to discuss the issue. He also invited the community each evening at the end of the community meal to go to the Shrine of St. Joseph at a side altar of the church and recite the Litany of St. Joseph for the successful outcome of the Vancouver proposal.[12] The chapter eventually met on August 5, 1939, and gave approval for the Canadian foundation. On September 5, five monks were blessed and sent to Ladner, British Columbia. This new foundation had a somewhat complicated birthing process that will be treated later, but the decision to embark on the project served as yet another signal of the growing confidence of the community for its future.

On January 10, 1937, Abbot Thomas blessed the new gymnasium that was erected for the student body. It was partially the result of efforts made by Mount Angel through the local WPA (Works Progress Administration) to develop programs for community improvement.[13] This coincided with a marked increase in the enrollment of all the schools and a change of organization initiated by Abbot Thomas. In 1939 he created a separate administration of the college and the seminary. Father James Koessler was appointed head of the college, and Fr. Damian Jentges was made rector of the seminary.

Just as Abbot Thomas manifested a new concern for the living conditions of the brothers, he recognized that the Benedictine sisters working on the hilltop deserved a better residence than their cramped quarters in the loft of the post office building. A house next to the abbey kitchen was built for them and served as a far more appropriate space for the sisters, faithfully assisting the monks of Mount Angel.

There was an effort by Abbot Thomas in this period to have Mount Angel break some of its geographical isolation. It hosted the General

---

12. *Abbey Chronicle* XXXV, 5. After the foundation in British Columbia was made, it was placed under the patronage of St. Joseph. Moreover, the tradition of the monastic community today to recite the Litany of St. Joseph after their evening meal each day dates from this time.

13. The gymnasium construction was also aided by the friendship Fr. Alcuin Heibel had cemented with Harry Hopkins, national head of the WPA, and the Oregon WPA head, Mr. E. J. Griffith.

Chapter of the Swiss-American Congregation in the summer of 1938 and the American Benedictine Educational Convention in 1939. A number of the abbots and visiting Benedictines who had responded generously to the financial appeals of Mount Angel after the fire the previous decade could now see and admire the fruits of that generosity. In turn, Mount Angel monks were made to see in these visitors a sampling of the resources they shared with fellow American Benedictines. Abbot Thomas for his part encouraged members of the community to affiliate with national Benedictine organizations such as the American Benedictine Academy and feel their connection to the greater Benedictine Order.

From Depression to War

One of the advantages of Mount Angel's close connection with the European continent was a high degree of awareness of how troubled the political situation had become by the late 1930s. Abbot Thomas made an extensive tour of different European countries when he traveled for the Abbots' Congress of 1937 and was in contact with abbots who lived under fascist regimes in Germany and Italy. The turmoil hit closer to home when, in the fall of 1939, Abbot Thomas communicated to the Abbot Primate that Fr. Thomas Brockhaus, slated to finish studies for a doctorate in canon law in Rome, was being called home, given the invasion of Poland by Hitler's Germany on September 1, and the subsequent declaration of war by Europe's Allied nations against Germany and Italy.

The conflict in Europe was beginning to have its effects in Oregon, too. In March of 1940, Mount Angel provided a temporary refuge for Fr. Romuald Edenhofer, a monk of Metten Abbey in Germany. An opponent of the Nazi party, he escaped to the United States and saw in Mount Angel a welcome place where he could have a Benedictine environment and freedom to live out his vocation. Edenhofer stayed in Mount Angel for the duration of the war, teaching in the seminary and becoming editor of the *St. Josephs Blatt*.[14] Two months

---

14. "Founders Find a New Site," *Abbey Chronicle* XXXVI, 6. Edenhofer eventually became a US citizen and prevailed upon his abbot at Metten to continue to live at Mount Angel until his death in 1958.

earlier the chapter had approved a temporary residence at the abbey for Fr. Gregory Sorger, a monk of Beuron from its priory in Japan, who sought a haven from the turmoil of his own country and its Asian Axis friend.[15] Hospitality was offered by the monastic chapter in 1943 to a monk of the Abbey of Maria Laach in Germany, Albert Hammenstede. Father Albert had come to know many of the monks of Mount Angel who had visited him in Germany, and now these monks were happy to return the favor.

Father Albert and a confrere from Maria Laach, Fr. Damasus Winzen, had been sent to the United States in the late 1930s for the un-publicized purpose of seeking a place for a possible American refuge for their monastery in case the Nazi regime of Hitler closed Maria Laach. Given the similar circumstances that had prompted Engelberg Abbey to make its American foundations over a half-century earlier, Mount Angel was quite sympathetic to their plight. Thus in 1939, the Mount Angel chapter gave their assent to a letter from Fr. Damasus Winzen requesting hospitality from abbeys in the United States.[16] Father Damasus was also a close friend of Fr. Luke Eberle. They began corresponding again during the war and kept up that correspondence after the war, when Fr. Damasus decided to put down roots in the United States and become founder and first superior of the monastery of Mount Saviour in Elmira, New York.

Indeed, Mount Angel acquired the reputation of being a sanctuary for monks from Axis countries who did not feel it was safe to return home. In this regard, it was a visiting Austrian monk who led the famous Von Trapp family to make a trip to Mount Angel during the war years and initiate a friendship with Abbot Thomas and the monks that lasted well beyond the end of World War II.

Unlike the circumstances at the close of World War I when it was forced to discontinue publishing, the *St. Josephs Blatt* now became a preferred piece of reading material, whose copies were purchased by the US government for many of the German POWs held in US camps, an ironic turnaround that must have prompted satisfaction to many who worked in the Press.

15. Chapter minutes of January 8, 1940.
16. Chapter minutes of January 24, 1939.

Abbot Thomas Meier and the Von Trapp family on a visit to Mount Angel,
February 24, 1942.

With the bombing of Pearl Harbor in December of 1941 and
American entry into the war, life at Mount Angel took another turn.
Like all states bordering the Pacific Ocean, there was an added sense
of vulnerability felt in the first years of the war. The monastic community was alerted to this new reality with the required blackout in
force from midnight until 8:00 a.m. Given how much of the monastic
schedule was centered in the hours from 5:00 to 8:00 a.m., there was
a need for considerable alteration of schedule. Morning Divine Office
took place in the chapter room. The daily Conventual Mass took place
at 7:30 a.m. in the abbey church. There was limited light, however,
especially on winter mornings. The seminarians were allowed to sleep
until 7:00 a.m., instead of the accustomed 5:20 a.m. The monastery
and seminary kitchens were asked to cooperate in the food-rationing
program, although the fact that much of the food was grown on the
property made government regulations less burdensome than that
endured by other institutions.

Students did their part, including collecting scrap metal and co-
operating with the blackout. The college and seminary hung a service
flag of 254 stars in Aquinas Hall, displaying the over 200 alumni who

were on active duty in branches of the US Armed Forces. The school schedule changed, too. Summer vacation was eliminated, and in the war years there were summer sessions between June and September. The number of young men entering the Armed Forces greatly affected the college enrollment. Only seminarians stayed on campus after 1942.[17] In retrospect, one is impressed at how a rhythm of normalcy was kept intact both in the monastery and in the schools. The war effort engaged the hilltop on all levels, and, like their fellow citizens, the monastic community and the student population showed a willingness to make sacrifices for the common good.

A striking example of this among the monks was a reawakening of a tradition started in World War I of community members volunteering for service as chaplains in the Armed Forces. In 1943 Fr. Bertrand McLaughlin left for Harvard to attend chaplain school. In that same year Fr. Hildebrand Melchior began service as chaplain in the Oregon National Guard. Priest-monks of the abbey provided sacramental assistance to the nearby army camps. Camp Adair, north of Corvallis, had eleven different chapels on the base and three to four monks from Mount Angel would travel there regularly for sacramental supply. In the summer months some of the abbey's older monks were enlisted to help with the agricultural work in the fields in absence of some of the lay help who ordinarily would do such work but now were involved in the war effort.

The spirit of sacrifice and self-restraint asked of all Americans during the war fit well into the texture of life in both the monastery and the school in the years from 1939 to 1945. Students took part in work details that scoured the abbey precincts for scrap metal. In the process, they discovered large mounds of scrap that were still present from the fire of 1926. There was cooperation with the limited rationing of food and fuel and the adjustments that had to be made in the school calendar. The fact that the abbey farms and schools, the parish work and the Benedictine Press, continued their work under trying condi-

---

17. "As the War Ends in Europe," *Abbey Chronicle* XLI, 5. By 1945 the graduation exercises were held in January rather than May or June, a sign that by this time the only remaining students were seminarians in the three-semester program.

tions was a testament to the constancy of purpose that had marked the previous half-century.

A New Vigor and Expansionism

As was the case with many other religious communities entrusted with institutions of higher education, the postwar period for Mount Angel was one of unprecedented promise and potential. One consensus that emerged in the chapter of Mount Angel as the war came to a close was that there had to be more space and buildings devoted to the seminary. This collective opinion developed in 1943–45, as numbers in the seminary increased. That increase had registered already before the war when young monks of St. Martin's Abbey in Lacey, Washington, began to do their seminary studies at Mount Angel. The increased numbers accelerated during the war because, among other reasons, the seminarians still received deferment in the draft. Moreover, the influx continued after the war, something experienced by other religious houses and seminaries as well, with numerous returning soldiers opting to discern a vocation to the religious life or priesthood. In September of 1946 the seminary enrollment jumped from fifty to eighty-one students.

Even though Abbot Thomas gave assurance in March of 1945 that he had no intention of discontinuing the college after the war, it was clear that it would have to be a college that was responsive to the sweeping changes in higher education.[18] The so-called GI Bill passed by Congress in 1944 provided funds for advanced education for all returning veterans and many were intent on going to college. Mount Angel had to come to terms with the intense competition among colleges in their geographic area. There were three Catholic colleges in Washington: the Jesuit schools at the University of Seattle and Gonzaga in Spokane, along with St. Martin's College in Lacey run by the American-Cassinese Benedictines. The Holy Cross Order ran the University of Portland. They all provided top-flight higher education, and they were all vying for students with the burgeoning state-run colleges in the vicinity. To add to the complications, government funds that poured into the state

18. Chapter minutes of March 7, 1945.

school system to administer the GI Bill put Mount Angel College at a disadvantage.

Many in the Mount Angel community sensed that decisions made on the nature and purpose of the community's educational apostolate would have a long-term impact on the monastery. Meanwhile, there was much intense discussion that took place in the community on the immediate need to expand the athletic facilities on campus and on the broader question of the future of the schools. In May of 1946, as a sign of how intense these matters were for the monastic chapter, at least four different community meetings that dealt with the issue of the abbey's educational apostolate took place.[19]

Some community members believed that the regular outside visitation of the community by Abbot Columban Thuis of St. Joseph Abbey in Louisiana in July of 1946 would bring some guidance on the question of the future of the schools. Although the visitor did not give any public indication of a preferred option, during the visitation there had surfaced on the part of a sizeable element in the community a desire to bring the matter to a head. Accordingly, shortly after Abbot Columban's departure, Abbot Thomas called a meeting of the abbey chapter. In that meeting he gave a definitive answer to the future direction of the schools. He stated that the intent in coming years would be to provide a seminary education only on the college and theology level:

> The first objective of our school from now on will be the Seminary and this means both a major and minor seminary. . . . After this definite decision and statement of school policy, I ask you not to discuss the school problem any further. If there are any suggestions in this regard to school policy, bring them directly to the Abbot or the rector of the school. Now that we have a definite objective let us all cooperate in realizing it.[20]

Even though there would be some non-seminary students in the high school, it was thought to be of little consequence.[21] Abbot Thomas, in line with the seminaries being run by St. Meinrad and Conception

---

19. *Abbey Chronicle* XLII (1946), 4.
20. *Abbey Chronicle* XLII, 5.
21. *Abbey Chronicle* XLI, 5.

monasteries, opted for that more exclusive seminary track. In this respect, Mount Angel was confirmed in its concentration of seminary education, much as its counterparts in the Swiss-American Congregation, St. Meinrad, Conception, and St. Joseph (Louisiana) were. Some also found congruence with the main mission of the community's first foundation in British Columbia, to undertake the administration of the major and minor seminary in that region. This decision on the primary purpose of the abbey's educational work was to prove pivotal in the future direction and identity that Mount Angel would have in the postwar years for the Northwest and beyond.

The decision coincided with the community's assent to build new athletic fields south of the hilltop and construct new buildings for a day high school. This was expedited by a number of purchases of buildings and material from War Assets or Surplus that were now made available at reasonable prices by the government. In 1946 and early 1947, the abbey chapter approved four new building units that became the basis for the new day high school that opened in the fall of 1947 and a gymnasium for the seminary.[22] This proved to be an economically viable course that allowed for the seminary and the high school to continue to grow in the postwar years.

Alcuin Heibel and the Mission to Mexico

One of the figures that played an outsized role in Mount Angel's history during these years was Fr. Alcuin Heibel. A native Minnesotan, Heibel was ordained to the priesthood in 1921. As a cleric, he was sent to the University of Oregon to learn how to develop curricula for the college.[23] That may have been one of the reasons why Abbot Bernard Murphy appointed him as rector of the college at the ripe age of twenty-five. Father Alcuin was the person most responsible for shepherding the college through the difficult years after the fire of 1926 and securing its accreditation. In those same years he was the person most responsible

---

22. *Abbey Chronicle* XLIII (1946–47), 6–7.
23. Father Alcuin Heibel was one of the first Mount Angel monks sent to state universities in the United States for graduate work. He later received his MA in history from Columbia University.

for raising funds for the new building program. He was appointed spiritual director of retreats by Archbishop Howard in 1928 and retained that position until 1944.[24] With the election of Abbot Thomas in 1934, Fr. Alcuin was appointed as pastor of the parish of St. Mary's in Mt. Angel. In the midst of the Great Depression, he won acclaim for his cooperative work with the Protestant ministers of the area in distributing food and necessities to poor families. Because of his friendship with national figures such as Harry Hopkins, an advisor to President Franklin Roosevelt and head of the Works Progress Administration, Fr. Alcuin was instrumental in obtaining funds for the construction of the gymnasium that was erected in 1937.

In 1935 Fr. Alcuin made a visit to Mexico. This was a response to a personal call that he had felt since his days as a youth when he felt a special solidarity with Catholics in Mexico who were imperiled by the anticlerical revolution of 1912–1921. In 1930, Fr. Alcuin wrote to the Archbishop of Guadalajara. He proposed inviting Mexican seminarians and a priest to come to Mount Angel. There they would be given an opportunity to pray and work as they continued their studies, with the hope of establishing a monastic community in Mexico. It was a vision he shared with Abbot Bernard.[25] The cultivation of this idea was singular in design and implementation. There was no invitation from Catholics in Mexico, nor a mandate from monks at Mount Angel. When Fr. Alcuin left on his journey to Mexico in 1935, his vision had expanded to a more adventurous goal, searching for a rural locale where he might be able to start a monastic community that combined cooperative agricultural work with the local population and a monastic schedule. It is hard to calculate what manner of support Fr. Alcuin had in all of this from his superior at that time, Abbot Thomas, or from the larger Mount Angel community, but the fact that he received permission to go seems to attest that they recognized the authentic zeal that was behind the excursion. For his part, Fr. Alcuin must have known of the high-risk nature of his solo missionary trip to Mexico. At the time of his exploratory journey in 1935, priests were not allowed to appear

24. *Mount Angel Letter* (April 1970), 2.

25. Letter of Alcuin Heibel to Abbot Bernard Murphy, September 12, 1930, MAAA. The plan was not at the point of being realized at the time.

in clerical dress in Mexico and the suspicions about his project must have been part of the hazards of his expedition, but he was not daunted. He completed his reconnaissance of possible sites and remained committed to starting a mission in Mexico.

On his return, it seems that Abbot Thomas tried to dissuade Fr. Alcuin from carrying out such a mission in the name of Mount Angel. So Fr. Alcuin then turned to Abbot Alcuin Deutsch of St. John's Abbey in Minnesota and asked if he could send monks for such a project.[26] When Abbot Alcuin responded that he could not spare Collegeville monks for such an exploratory foundation at that time, Fr. Alcuin was not deterred. He requested of Abbot Thomas permission to return to Mexico in the spring of 1942, with the intention of considering sites for an experimental farm in conjunction with a monastery. In this enterprise, too, Fr. Alcuin was well connected. He established close friendships with Monsignor Luigi Ligutti, head of the National Catholic Rural Life Conference, and Bishop Edwin O'Hara of Kansas City, Missouri. He also sought the assistance of Abbot Martin Veth of St. Benedict's Abbey in Atchison, Kansas.

One other factor seemed to make this renewed effort propitious. By 1943, Fr. Alcuin had been relieved of his duties as pastor in Mt. Angel and was able to concentrate more intensely on the Mexican project. He decided to center the new foundation in a rural area of Suhuayo, Michoacan. However, there were a series of problems that still faced Fr. Alcuin. Under the government's laws, a church entity was not allowed to have property in Mexico under its name. Along with that, there remained the inevitable question of finding adequate personnel to staff such a new monastic foundation. The latter was alleviated somewhat when a number of monks from Atchison were given permission to take part in the mission. The idealism of the project is seen in Fr. Alcuin's vision of a monastic community that would enjoy rural life with the peasant population and yet preach and be in contact with the wider faith community.[27] He saw it as carrying on the missionary tradition of the Benedictine Congregation of St. Ottilien and as

---

26. Letter of Fr. Alcuin Heibel to Abbot Alcuin Deutsch, November 11, 1940, MAAA.

27. Letter of Fr. Alcuin Heibel to Abbot Thomas Meier, July 24, 1944, MAAA.

fulfilling his youthful design to come to the assistance of beleaguered Catholics in Mexico.

Even as the Suhuayo project was still in flux, Fr. Alcuin visited Mexico City and a school there in Tepeyac that was in need of staffing. In response to this need, he turned to the Benedictine community of women in Atchison, Kansas, under Mother Lucy Dooley. By 1944 he saw that there were sisters from that community in place. They became the basis for what would become the school and eventually the monastic community of Tepeyac.[28] Almost thirty years after this effort, shortly after the community of Tepeyac had become an abbey, a confrere of Fr. Alcuin, Fr. Ambrose Zenner, wrote to the first abbot of Tepeyac, Placid Reitmeier, reminding him that the true founder of Tepeyac was Fr. Alcuin and that he merited recognition for that status in the eyes of history.[29]

Meanwhile, Fr. Alcuin sought assistance from the Swiss-American Congregation and its monasteries to provide monks for the Suhuayo project, but to no avail. With all of the demands made on communities as the war was drawing to its close, it was not an opportune time to be in search for capable personnel to be directed to another country.

Requests for assistance became a moot question when Fr. Alcuin received a letter from Abbot Thomas in late 1944, recalling him from Mexico and appointing him as pastor of Sacred Heart Church in Portland.[30] Even though Fr. Alcuin was by this time questioning the feasibility of the Suhuayo project, he was severely disappointed at the news of his new appointment. He reluctantly acceded to the abbot's wishes and returned to Oregon in January of 1945, still believing that his projected Benedictine community in Mexico was more than a flight of fancy.

The bold and singular plan of Fr. Alcuin's Mexican enterprise invites sustained reflection. One can speak of Fr. Alcuin's initial foray south of the border as a pathfinding expedition for the eventual founda-

28. The Atchison monks who came to Mexico to assist Fr. Alcuin eventually went to Tepeyac. When they decided to return to Kansas in 1946, Abbot Alcuin Deutsch was persuaded by Fr. Alcuin to take over the school and community under the aegis of St. John's Abbey.

29. Letter of Fr. Ambrose Zenner to Abbot Placid Reitmeier of Tepeyac, January 6, 1972, MAAA.

30. Letter of Abbot Thomas to Fr. Alcuin, November 18, 1944, MAAA.

tion of Mount Angel in Mexico that came over two decades later. But perhaps a better understanding of Fr. Alcuin's unique and innovative role is contained in a letter sent by a fellow American educator and missionary to Abbot Thomas: "In my more than nine years of residence in Mexico, I have met no other American who learned so much about Mexico in such a short period of time as Fr. Alcuin had needed to accomplish the great good that can be credited to him up to now."[31] Joined to this encomium is one delivered by Fr. Alcuin's close friend, Bishop O'Hara of Kansas City, who went so far as to write to Abbot Thomas, trying to persuade him to change his mind in calling back Fr. Alcuin to the United States: "While there can be found one hundred men who are able and certainly willing to become pastor of a city parish in Portland, there has not appeared a single other priest in the U.S. except Father Alcuin who has the qualifications and the willingness to undertake the important mission for the Church in Mexico."[32] What is beyond question is that Fr. Alcuin's sense of vision, leadership, and personal zeal were all recognized and applauded by peers who worked with him during his time in Mexico. Furthermore, the combination of his presence and contacts in that country can be said to have laid the groundwork for a future foundation of Mount Angel.

Servicing the Needs of Refugees

Father Alcuin's return to Oregon in 1945 coincided with the end of World War II. One of the most pressing problems facing the war-torn European continent was the large number of refugees displaced by the war. In partial response to this, Abbot Thomas appointed Fr. Alcuin as head of the Central European Relief Committee, to be assisted by Fr. Francis Burger, then head of the Benedictine Press. Father Alcuin took the lead in encouraging his fellow monks and others to help in the distribution of food and clothes to those who were most needy in Austria and Germany. As he wrote to the abbot president of the Swiss-

31. Letter of Paul V. Murray of the American School Foundation to Abbot Thomas, December 3, 1944, MAAA.

32. Letter of Bishop Edwin O'Hara to Abbot Thomas Meier, December 12, 1944, MAAA.

American Congregation: "The monasteries in Europe started us in the United States. Now we in the United States must in turn save the monasteries of Europe."[33]

This was to be the start of a work that brought Fr. Alcuin and Mount Angel into a global landscape of social justice and charitable works. Key to the success of this effort was Fr. Alcuin's remarkable network of personal connections. He was enlisted by the National Catholic Relief Services (under Monsignor Patrick O'Boyle in Washington, DC) to work in tandem with them as he headed overseas.

Father Alcuin traveled in these postwar years throughout war-torn Europe, speaking on behalf of the European refugees and helping to organize the aid effort. In a twist of status, some of the very Benedictine houses in German-speaking countries that had afforded hospitality and resources to the monks of Mount Angel in the first decades of the twentieth century, such as Beuron, Maria Laach, St. Peter's in Salzburg, and Saint Boniface in Munich, now became the beneficiaries of the largesse of Fr. Alcuin's relief committee as they recovered from the ravages of World War II.

The Mount Angel monastic community also took a personal stake in this effort by hosting a number of displaced persons at the abbey from 1949 on. They offered them employment and a supportive environment for their families, and the project was deemed a success. This was largely due to the intensive efforts of Fr. Alcuin, who recognized that providing a haven for displaced persons on the hilltop would be both a gesture of Benedictine hospitality and a means of added revenue to the abbey.[34] The movement of the displaced persons was triggered by an appearance that Fr. Alcuin made on behalf of Archbishop Howard before a Congressional Committee in Washington, DC, in March of 1949, yet another unprecedented witness by a Mount Angel monk in a national public forum.

33. Letter of Fr. Alcuin Heibel to Abbot Columban Thuis, December 10, 1945, MAAA.

34. See letter of Fr. Alcuin to Abbot Thomas, January 26, 1949, MAAA. Beginning in 1949, Mount Angel did receive a number of displaced persons, some of whom transitioned to other jobs and a few of whom stayed on for some years, working at the abbey.

Fr. Alcuin Heibel with Pope Paul VI in Rome in September 1973.

Father Alcuin did his utmost to persuade the Mount Angel monks to foster a wider perspective on world events. He made a rather convincing case for this in a letter he sent to Abbot Thomas from Sacred Heart Parish in Portland in early 1949:

> Because of my own experiences I am definitely an "internationalist." I feel that it is not "un-Benedictine" because the Order is as broad as the Church. I shall always work for the local autonomy of our abbeys, but equally I shall always work "against" provincialism of our abbeys in a time when the "entire Benedictine Order" has to stand together to help the Church, in a time when the Benedictines should again take their part in this world crisis. I have said so often that Asia was not yet ours (although it is the future of the world). . . . Now comes this opportunity in Europe where I feel that I could again be of real service.[35]

Father Alcuin had his wish fulfilled when Abbot Primate Bernard Kaelin called him to Rome in May of 1950, and, in conjunction with the Vatican Secretariat of State, he was commissioned to travel to

---

35. Letter of Fr. Alcuin Heibel to Abbot Thomas Meier, January 26, 1949, MAAA.

Germany and Austria to study the conditions of war refugees there. Abbot Thomas freed Fr. Alcuin for the task. This coincided with Fr. Alcuin's reception of the *Pro Ecclesia et Pontifice* papal medal presented by Archbishop Howard in recognition for his work on May 1, 1950.

In the early years of the 1950s Fr. Alcuin used the *Mount Angel Letter* as an effective tool for disseminating news of his efforts in Europe and creating a deeper sense of solidarity for the displaced persons of World War II. He also forged relationships with American governmental officials and church contacts, not the least of which was Archbishop Giovanni Montini, the future Pope Paul VI, in Milan. The archbishop was so impressed with the immediate impact of Fr. Alcuin on the refugees in his archdiocese that he gave him full use of a car and material resources. In later years, when Montini became Pope, he was pleased to visit with his friend from Mount Angel.

The friendship that developed with the future Roman Pontiff in Milan was illustrative of the gift for networking that Fr. Alcuin only sharpened through the remainder of his life. In many ways, the wealth of relationships that Fr. Alcuin forged and fostered during his many years away from the monastery strengthened and expanded the spiritual fabric of Mount Angel in ways few could have anticipated.

Modifications and Movement Forward

With the end of the war, Abbot Thomas expressed his desire to bring back certain practices and adapt others. The tradition of sending monks away to Europe for studies would be reinstated.[36] Given the demands of administration and teaching that were steadily increasing, there was in addition a noticeable plan to send monks to quality schools in the United States. Monks were sent not only to the iconic institutions of Catholic higher education such as the Catholic University of America and the University of Notre Dame, but to Fordham and Harvard, Stanford and UCLA.

The Scripture reading that was daily proclaimed in the refectory was changed from Latin to English. This was to benefit the lay brothers, but it was also met with positive acceptance by the priest-monks.

36. Chapter minutes for March 7, 1945.

In 1948 the statue of St. Joseph that was formerly in the church was moved to the monastic refectory, an appropriate place given the ongoing practice of praying the Litany of St. Joseph after the evening meal every day. Devotion to St. Joseph remained a mainstay of the spiritual life of the monastery.

In July of 1945 Abbot Thomas asked the chapter to endorse his plan to hire an architect to draw up plans for a new abbey church. Abbot Thomas was intent upon seeing the church come into being before he would leave office. Dating back to 1922, a special fund had been created for donations to construct a church. Over twenty years later, there was sufficient money to cover costs of an architect and initial building. In December of 1949 the abbey chapter voted to begin building the church. It was to be the crown jewel of the building program for Abbot Thomas and the fulfillment of the dream of Abbot Bernard to have an abbey church whose dimensions and monastic ambience would be a tribute to the best of the Benedictine tradition.

Pursuant to the decision to separate the high school and the college and theology seminary levels, a new day high school was put up through housing units secured from War Assets. On September 22, 1947, Abbot Thomas presided at a Pontifical Mass to inaugurate the high school.

In November of 1947, there was a subtle modification of the community's corporate identity. From early in its history, the formal title of the community had been St. Benedict's Abbey.[37] Since there were a number of different abbeys in the world with that same name, Abbot Thomas recommended that the corporate title of the abbey be changed to Mount Angel Abbey. It was done so in 1947 and remains so to this day.

Change was also coming from within the monastic ranks. Father Victor was forced to step down as choirmaster because of ill health. His replacement was Fr. Dennis Marx. Father Dennis had studied at Juilliard in New York City and in Toronto and had visited Solesmes to learn chant. He was an able successor for Fr. Victor, upholding the high standards of liturgical music. It was at this time that the music departments of the University of Oregon in Eugene and Willamette University

---

37. So, too, the official name of the post office was Saint Benedict—and not Mount Angel.

in Salem invited the seminary to present a program on Gregorian chant. Father Justin Reilly, the rector of the seminary, agreed and under the guidance of Fr. David Nicholson, the new seminary choirmaster, the request was heeded. The choir appeared at the two university venues and at St. Mary's Academy in Portland to enthusiastic reviews.[38]

By 1950 the signs of financial stability in the community were most welcome. After having lived with crushing indebtedness and fiscal uncertainty for much of their history, Mount Angel could point to several factors that had helped to let them face the demands of postwar expansion with new optimism. The increased presence of priests in the parishes brought an increase in revenue for sacramental help. That was the case both for parishes that were entrusted to the abbey such as Sacred Heart in Portland and for those where the monks of the abbey provided part-time service. The timber lands acquired so assiduously over the years were an ongoing source of profit. In this sector the monastery displayed a practiced ecological sensibility. The monastery implemented a program of judicious reforestation after select cuttings, maintaining the beauty and the ecological balance of the timber areas at the base of the Cascades east of the abbey.[39] The Press continued to be a source of revenue, largely due to the still robust numbers of monastic members who were in its employ. Apart from the yearly crops of grain, corn, hay, and hops, the farm's beef and dairy herds provided meat and milk not only for the community but also for surplus that was sold to the local creamery. The surplus pork from the hog farms also constituted a profit-making venture. There was, in addition, the equivalent of a giant farmers' market each year from the abbey's orchards (apples, cherries, peaches, and pears) and the walnut trees, berries, and vegetables grown on abbey land. The mid-twentieth century was the high-water mark for such efficient monastic economy. The combination of dwindling monastic manpower, accelerating technological innovation, and changing tax laws would render this monastic model obsolete within another generation as will be seen in an analysis of the 1970s.

---

38. *Abbey Chronicle* XLVIII (1951), 5.

39. Lawrence McCrank, *Mt. Angel Abbey: A Centennial History of the Benedictine Community and Its Library, 1882–1982* (Wilmington, DE: Scholarly Resources, 1983), 78.

A New Abbot and New Confidence

Two abbatial predecessors of Abbot Thomas, Thomas Meienhofer and Bernard Murphy, had both made a decision to step down from their office in part because of medically serious eye conditions. By 1950, Abbot Thomas Meier realized that his vision and his entire physical condition had reached a critical point. During a hospital stay in Portland in Holy Week of that year, a hemorrhage in one eye caused his doctors to recommend that he consider removing himself from all leadership responsibilities to ease his stress. Abbot Thomas and the members of the community concurred with the recommendation of the physicians.[40] This led to a petition being sent to Rome requesting that the community at Mount Angel elect a coadjutor abbot, one who would take over the administration and governance of the abbey, the same manner of election that had taken place in 1934. There was a trying period of waiting for the petition to be returned. Once the permission was received from Rome, a date was set for the election, August 16, 1950. The community elected on the first ballot Fr. Damian Jentges as coadjutor and fifth abbot of Mount Angel.

Abbot Damian was of Luxembourger heritage, an identity he honored by regular visits to that country when he was in Europe. Though he was born in Kansas, he spent most of his early years in Idaho. It was from there that he learned about Mount Angel and entered the seminary and later the abbey. He was the last of the leaders of the community to have been on the scene when the fire of 1926 leveled the hilltop. He was one more example of the European-educated monk. He had received a doctorate in moral theology from the University of Salzburg. When he returned to Mount Angel from his studies in Europe in 1931, he taught in the seminary and also served the community as subprior, choirmaster, and guest master, eventually becoming dean and rector of the seminary. He served as spiritual director of the laymen's retreat guild and was responsible for hosting retreats at Mount Angel for various groups. From 1945 to the time of his election, he was

---

40. *Abbey Chronicle* XLVI (1950), 7. Abbot Thomas spent most of the spring and summer of 1950 recuperating at the home of a family member in California. He eventually recovered and returned to Mount Angel, living another decade and dying in 1961.

Abbot Damian Jentges prostrate in the sanctuary at his abbatial
blessing, October 10, 1950.

pastor at St. Mary's Parish in Mt. Angel. All of these roles ensured that
Abbot Damian would have a wide familiarity with the life and work
of the abbey.

Abbot Damian took over a community of eighty-four members.
There were fifty-six priest members of the community, nine clerics
studying for the priesthood, and roughly twenty brothers. He was
witness to the surge in enrollment that was taking place in the abbey's
schools and in the monastic community itself. There had been a slow
but perceptible increase in numbers for both the seminary and the monastic community in the decades after the war. Abbot Damian was to
be a beneficiary of this surge as he opened new doors in the outreach
of the abbey.

A reliable marker of the personal views and accomplishments of
Abbot Damian is the *Mount Angel Letter*. Published as "a newsletter
to our friends and benefactors," this publication of the Press took on
a higher profile in the years when Abbot Damian was superior. He
opened his mind on events relating to the monastery and the seminary in his regular letter that occupied the front page of each issue. It
became something of a template for the mission of the abbey as it was
projected and articulated by Abbot Damian over the next two decades.

Abbot Damian turning ground for Anselm Hall, January 4, 1954.

The first challenge of the new abbot was to complete the building program begun by his predecessor and to extend it to other parts of the hilltop campus. The abbey church's central nave and crypt were completed and blessed after several years of construction.[41] The formal blessing of Abbot Damian took place on March 21, 1952. It seemed fitting that the prelate presiding at the blessing was Archbishop Howard, who had seen firsthand and blessed all of the buildings constructed since the fire of 1926. Abbot Thomas, who had so perseveringly shepherded the plan for the church to its completion, was given the honor of serving as presiding abbot at the blessing.

Along with the community, Abbot Damian was pressed to make some decisions on material needs for the hilltop. The first of these was a decision to construct a new resident building for the seminary. The fact that all of the students for all twelve years of the seminary program were lodged in the one residence of Aquinas Hall, along with the prospect of even larger enrollment numbers, made this a necessity. Anselm Hall's construction was completed in 1954 and greatly eased the crunch for resident space. Landscape architects enhanced the beauty of the campus and established a plan for a connecting road on the hilltop and a vision of building for the future. Father Matthias Burger was placed

41. McCrank, *Mt. Angel Abbey*, 70.

in charge of the landscaping improvements and many of the younger monks lent their hands to the challenge of beautification of the campus. There was now an array of flowers, fountains, trees, and shrubs that framed the new buildings in a way previously not seen. California sequoia trees made their first appearance.[42] One other new fixture that appeared in these years was Our Lady of Tikhvin Center, a remodeled chapel, converted from the former residence of the Benedictine sisters, that ministered to the Old Believers Russian community long resident in the area around the monastery.

Abbot Damian employed his own version of strategic planning before that term became part of the community lexicon. As he took over the reins of leadership, he sensed the potential for growth of Mount Angel's monastic and ministerial presence. However, his personal prudence and his desire to avoid the indebtedness that had been so much a part of Mount Angel's previous history prompted him to use caution. One of the great advantages that coincided with Abbot Damian's first years in office was the opportunity to empower a number of his most talented monks in positions of responsibility and influence. Most of these individuals had experienced in their formative years the testing time of the previous few decades of the fire of 1926 and its aftermath, the deprivation of the country's Great Depression, the involvement in a global war, and the struggle to obtain a corporate financial foothold free of indebtedness. It is to some of these monks that one can now turn so as to better insert them in the story of Mount Angel's maturation in the middle of the twentieth century.

Martin Pollard

Father Martin Pollard came to Mount Angel by way of two different countries. Born in England in 1902, his family moved to Canada in 1912. They eventually settled in Victoria, British Columbia, where he became a seminarian for that diocese and came to Mount Angel in 1920 as a student. He was attracted to the life of the abbey and was received into the novitiate on September 7, 1926.[43] He experienced the fire of 1926 and shortly after making his first profession in September of 1927 was sent to Rome. Remarkably, he did not pursue first theo-

---

42. *Abbey Chronicle* LII (1956), 2.
43. Necrology of Mount Angel Abbey, February 8, 1997.

logical studies for the priesthood but instead obtained a doctorate in philosophy at Sant'Anselmo. He then continued his theological studies at Sant'Anselmo and was ordained to the priesthood in 1932. Most fittingly, he made his solemn profession at the Abbey of Engelberg on September 8, 1930.

He returned to the abbey in 1933, a prototype of the Rome-educated and European-traveled monks of Mount Angel. He taught in the seminary and served as both subprior and novice master before being named prior by Abbot Thomas in 1946. As a sign of Abbot Damian's respect for Fr. Martin's service as prior, he retained him

Fr. Martin Pollard, prior under Abbot Damian.

in his position as prior in 1950, and Fr. Martin remained in that post until 1971. Few communities could match the record of an uninterrupted quarter-century of service in the demanding position of prior. He was a man of unparalleled energy and unmistakable monasticity. He helped to maintain the liturgical standards of the abbey and found himself over the years to be the chronicler of the abbey's history. His meticulous and personal yearly chronicles of abbey life in the *Mount Angel Letter* were treasured by many readers.

During the course of his tenure as teacher in the seminary, students gave Fr. Martin the moniker *Ens Mobile,* Latin for "a being in motion." It was an affectionate nickname that captured the irrepressible nature of some of his lectures when he was known to jump on the top of his desk to emphasize a point. It also seemed fitting that the monk who embodied so much of European monastic tradition would never learn to drive a car but still travel in mind and in company with others to all corners of the monastic world.

As someone who was associated with tried and true monastic tradition and practices, many were surprised at the alacrity with which Fr. Martin became an advocate of many of the reforms associated with the Second Vatican Council. In a series of letters he wrote to Fr. Andrew Baumgartner in 1964, Fr. Martin heralded the use of English in the liturgical life of the community. He was a member of the Abbey Liturgical Commission and was a zealous advocate of concelebration. No doubt he saw that much of the pioneering liturgical experiments he had come to know when he was at Maria Laach in Germany as a student were now being incorporated into the mainstream of liturgical life. Father Martin was also one of the first Mount Angel monks to promote ecumenical dialogue, with local Protestant clergy being invited to the hilltop for dialogue during his time as prior in the 1960s.

Many of his articles for the *Mount Angel Letter* over four decades display the widespread familiarity he had with themes of Benedictine spirituality and his remarkable ability to draw from the repository of Mount Angel's past. Father Martin's counsel for several generations of abbots and his familiarity with the community history were invaluable assets to those wishing to tap these sources. His love for the community of Mount Angel and his example of monastic observance served as a pillar for the community in its formative stages in the twentieth century.

Father Martin became a mentor for many seminarians and monks. He inculcated especially his love of learning and of the richness of monastic tradition through his distinctive blend of exuberance and discipline. He combined a refinement in intellectual and cultural life with a practical understanding of the daily flow of cloistered life. If there was a primer to employ for how to pass from European to American monastic customs, from the church of pre-Vatican II to the church of post-Vatican II, Fr. Martin was the person to write it. His lived pedagogy of how to be a monk was a gift readily welcomed by those fortunate enough to encounter it.

LUKE EBERLE

Father Luke Eberle's family had its roots from German-Russian stock in North Dakota, but he came to live in the town of Mt. Angel when he was a boy. His large family is emblematic of so many others of his time. Two of his sisters became members of the Queen of Angels Convent, and his brother was professed as Br. Benedict at Mount Angel. His nephew, Peter, would later become abbot of the community. Fr. Luke Eberle spent his high school years and his first two years of college at the seminary and then entered the novitiate in 1930. Only one year later, he was sent to Europe to complete his years of college study and learn how to play the pipe organ. He did this at the Abbey of Maria Laach in Germany, where he came into contact with Abbot Idelfonse Herwegen, a luminary in the Liturgical Movement. He also spent time at the Abbey of Clervaux in Luxembourg, where he made friends with and served as unofficial English tutor for Fr. Jean Leclercq, a monk who was to become perhaps the foremost scholar on Benedictine spirituality and history in the second half of the twentieth century. These rich experiences with European monasticism were to leave their mark for several generations of monks

Fr. Luke Eberle cutting grass in front of the abbey.

at Mount Angel in subsequent years. It is most revealing that Fr. Luke kept in contact with figures from these European monastic centers over the entire span of his monastic life, most notably Frs. Leclercq and Damasus Winzen of Maria Laach. These two monks were arguably two of the most influential mid-century figures in the Benedictine world, and they both sought the wisdom and counsel of Fr. Luke.

When he returned from Europe in 1934, he professed his solemn vows, completed his studies for the priesthood, and began training generations of organists at the abbey. He was also associate editor and editor of *St. Joseph Magazine* for eight years. He served as rector of the seminary and organist in the community for six years at the new foundation of Mount Angel in British Columbia. His return to Mount Angel in 1950 coincided with Abbot Damian's election. Abbot Damian named him novice master, and Fr. Luke was to remain in that position for the next fourteen years, helping to shape spiritually a generation of monks who would play vital roles in the history of the abbey. In addition, Fr. Luke can qualify as one of the monk-scholars of Mount Angel. He did his best to ensure that the abbey library would contain the finest sources in Benedictine spirituality, and he furthered the cause by completing the first English translation of the *Rule of the Master*, the monastic rule upon which St. Benedict largely derived his own. He brought together his affection for Engelberg and his scholarly bent when in 1973 he translated Abbot Leodegar Hunkeler of Engelberg's book on the origins of the Benedictine Order, *It Began With Benedict*. His translation of different German documents from the early history of Mount Angel was one more invaluable service he provided to the community.

As a sign of Fr. Luke's wide-ranging gifts and meticulousness, he spent fifteen years at the end of his life working in the abbey's business office as a bookkeeper and acquiring a reputation of someone whose work never had to be checked. In Fr. Luke's case, as in that of Fr. Martin's, his lived example served as his most valued legacy to the community. His faithfulness to the round of community life and his firm adherence to sound principles as a formator were treasured gifts.

Maybe one of the best articulations of Fr. Luke's monastic contribution came from the pen of the famed Benedictine scholar, Fr. Jean Leclercq. The correspondence between the two over several decades attests to their close friendship and mutual affection, notwithstanding their very different personalities. Father Jean was known for his many travels over the globe in the 1970s and '80s, while Fr. Luke was quite content to keep within the cloister of Mount Angel. Writing to Fr. Luke in 1978, Fr. Jean observed: "I'm a monastic misfit, but a happy one. You're the real monk. That is why I trust so much in your prayers for me. You do the real work; I play in a circus of illusions."[44] The certainty with which this monastic lecturer and expert on Benedictine spirituality could point to Fr. Luke as the "genuine article" of monastic life speaks most eloquently to the role Fr. Luke filled for many at Mount Angel.

Ambrose Zenner

Fr. Ambrose Zenner, like Abbot Damian, was of Luxembourger ancestry. Like Fr. Luke, his baptismal name was Joseph, and he came from a large family. All three of his sisters entered religious life and another of his brothers was ordained to the priesthood. Growing up in Oregon, he matriculated through the high school and college at Mount Angel and entered the monastery in 1941.[45] Shortly

---

44. Letter of Fr. Jean Leclercq to Fr. Luke Eberle, December 28, 1978, MAAA.
45. Necrology of Mount Angel Abbey, May 2, 1976.

Fr. Ambrose Zenner.

after his ordination in 1947, he was sent to the University of Notre Dame, where he absorbed much of the current of Catholic Action and lay participation that was at work in the American Catholic Church during that period. In 1948 he was sent to the University of Fribourg in Switzerland. After three years of study there, he was awarded a doctorate in theology, with specialization in church history and patristics. One of the advantages of his time in Switzerland as a student was the chance to spend extended periods of time at Engelberg Abbey. There he was given access to the archives, and with his linguistic gifts he transcribed large sections of Abbot Anselm Villiger's diary and other documents pertaining to Mount Angel's early history. His devotion to the community history of Mount Angel and his fondness for Engelberg were to have a positive and long-lasting effect on his fellow community members in Oregon.

Father Ambrose returned to Mount Angel in 1951. Abbot Damian placed him in the seminary to teach in 1951. The next year he was made vice-rector of the seminary and from 1954 to 1965 he served as rector. These were years when the seminary flourished in enrollment, and much of the credit for its growth can be attributed to his direction. Father Ambrose brought to these roles an industry and acumen that were recognized by peers and students alike. Abbot Damian relied on the advice and counsel of Fr. Ambrose. These qualities would be exemplified later when Abbot Damian entrusted him with leading the community's foundation in Mexico. The capable role he filled as the first superior of the community in Mexico will be treated at length later in the book.

Cardinal Basil Hume visited Mount Angel Abbey in September of 1982, some years after the death of Fr. Ambrose. Cardinal Hume had

been a classmate with Zenner at
the University of Fribourg in Switzerland. Commenting on his recollection of Fr. Ambrose as friend
and classmate, he said: "Father
Ambrose, though only two years
older, had an insight, compassion,
and understanding beyond his
age."[46] They are words that aptly
summarize the valued presence of
Fr. Ambrose at a critical period in
the history of Mount Angel.

THOMAS BROCKHAUS

Father Thomas Brockhaus, whose
Nebraska roots mirror many other
Mount Angel monks raised in that
section of the country, first came
to Mount Angel as a student in the

Fr. Thomas Brockhaus in front of abbey
church, 1989.

preparatory school three days before the fire of 1926. He later entered
Mount Angel Seminary and then the abbey. Father Thomas recounts
how when then Fr. Thomas Meier was his novice master, he was given
the works of Blessed Columba Marmion as the core of his monastic
formation and appreciated the depth it gave him in his further work
in liturgy and spirituality.[47] Father Thomas was ordained as a priest in
May of 1939. As previously noted, an intended program of theological
studies in Rome did not take place because of World War II. Instead, Fr.
Thomas was sent to the Catholic University of America in Washington,
DC, to study canon law. He studied under Fr. Louis Motry, a famed
canonist, and received his doctorate in canon law in 1947. Upon his
return to Mount Angel, Fr. Thomas became a fixture on the seminary
faculty, teaching canon law and three different language courses. He
was also associate editor of *St. Joseph Magazine* and served as master

46. Personal recollection of Fr. Augustine DeNoble, OSB, in 2018.

47. Interview given to Br. Cyril Drnjevic, OSB, December 31, 1998, transcript
in MAAA.

of ceremonies in 1943–58 and 1962–80. He also served as the secretary and chauffeur for Abbot Thomas. Abbot Damian regarded him highly as a community canonist to whom one could turn and receive a scholarly and correct response on any canonical question.[48] Father Thomas was a charter member of the Canon Law Society of America and of the Northwest Regional Canon Law Society.[49]

Father Thomas occupied a stalwart status for several important works of the monastery. He was a regular conductor of priest retreats that were given every summer. He gave ongoing spiritual talks to the community of Queen of Angels in Mt. Angel, and in the 1950s he spent several summers in Minnesota, teaching the Benedictine sisters at St. Benedict's Monastery. Within the Swiss-American Congregation, Fr. Thomas had the reputation of a canonical *peritus*. He delivered sound counsel on questions of canon law for both the Mount Angel community and monasteries of the Swiss-American Congregation. He was the first person elected to represent the community as a delegate at a General Chapter, serving in that capacity at the crucial chapter held at St. Joseph's Abbey in October of 1969 that dealt with the major agenda of monastic renewal. He was also the chair of the Mount Angel Liturgy Committee from 1977 to 1979.

Long after he retired from active teaching, Fr. Thomas remained a sought-after spiritual director and someone who was always a prime person from which to receive canonical consultation.

One other role performed by Fr. Thomas that is well documented in the *Mount Angel Letter* of the 1960s was as vice-postulator for the cause of the Italian Benedictine Sr. Fortunata Viti. He spent much time and energy promoting her cause and was privileged to go to Rome and Veroli, Italy, in the fall of 1967 for the beatification of Blessed Fortunata and relay firsthand accounts of the ceremony back to Mount Angel.

48. Prior to Fr. Thomas, Fr. Augustine Bachofen, as already noted, served as canonist and teacher for the abbey. After the death of Fr. Thomas, Fr. Paul Thomas became the community canonist and also served the congregation in that role.

49. See record of oral interview with Br. Cyril, December 31, 1998, MAAA. In 1988 Father Thomas received the Role of Law Award from the Canon Law Society of America, its highest honor.

BERNARD SANDER

Father Bernard Sander hailed from a large rural family in Tillamook, Oregon. He entered Mount Angel Abbey, making profession in September of 1939. He was ordained to the priesthood in 1944. In 1952 Abbot Damian made Fr. Bernard part of the administration of the seminary. He held administrative posts there for almost two decades and witnessed at close hand many of the seismic changes in the seminary that took place during that time.

Fr. Bernard Sander in 1954 photo.

A particular blessing that Fr. Bernard brought to the abbey and seminary was a time of study he had at the University of Notre Dame. At the urging of Fr. Ambrose, Fr. Bernard spent the summers of 1948 and 1949 at the University of Notre Dame and in Chicago. There he came under the influence of the notable Holy Cross priest, Fr. Louis Putz. Under the tutelage of Putz, Fr. Bernard came into contact with the CFM (Christian Family Movement), YCS (Young Catholic Students), and the YCW (Young Christian Workers). He developed friendships with such notable figures as Monsignor Reynold Hillenbrand, the former rector of Mundelein Seminary and a leader in the Liturgical Movement and Lay Apostolate, and Pat and Patricia Crowley, leaders of CFM.[50] Having fostered these personal contacts, Fr. Bernard invited other members of the YCW to come to the seminary and speak. The fact that such renowned figures as Monsignor Hillenbrand and Dorothy

---

50. Transcript of interview with Fr. Bernard Sander by Fr. Nathan Zodrow, OSB, Fall 1995, from the personal papers of Fr. Nathan. In this interview Fr. Bernard asserts that his time at Notre Dame opened him to the world of Catholic Action and the Lay Apostolate and helped him immensely with his seminary work and his later role as guest master and director of oblates.

Day of the *Catholic Worker* made stops at Mount Angel can be traced to the influence of Fr. Bernard. Abbot Damian gave permission for Fr. Bernard to travel to Europe in 1958 to attend an international meeting of YCW workers in Belgium. There he became friends with Rom Maione, an international leader of YCW. He also traveled to London and Paris. Upon his return, he made a point of involving the seminarians more deeply into issues of social justice and work with the laity. The summer conferences that took place at Mount Angel, beginning in the 1980s, were an offshoot of the work that Fr. Bernard did with the Christian Family Movement.

As mentioned above, Fr. Bernard was named as rector of the seminary in 1952 and stayed in that position until 1970, a remarkable span of years. Serving as rector of the minor seminary in the very turbulent era of the 1960s, Fr. Bernard acted as a buffer for seminarians pressing for more academic and pastoral options and the bishops who pressed their obligation to ensure doctrinal fidelity and personal discipline. At a juncture in the seminary's history when it was easy to fall into camps of liberal or conservative, Fr. Bernard was respected as a man who had the right combination of pastoral sensitivity and theological sensibleness.

Father Bernard was named guest master and retreat master for the community in 1970. It was in these two positions that he arguably had the most profound impact as a monk of Mount Angel. He served in these positions for over twenty years and touched the lives of many visitors who came to the hilltop. As a complement to his service of guests and retreatants, he was appointed oblate director in 1981 and revitalized the abbey's oblate program, developing the membership from about fifty to well over five hundred oblates at the end of his directorship. Under directors of oblates after him, the program remained vigorous, thanks to the solid core of lay men and women attracted by Fr. Bernard.

After his "retirement" as guest master, Fr. Bernard developed a Christian in the World program at the abbey, inviting noted Catholic speakers to give workshops on living out one's Christian vocation. A unique honor given to Fr. Bernard toward the end of his life was having the youth center in the town of Mt. Angel named after him, a fitting tribute to a life lived in service of the church.[51]

51. Necrology of Mount Angel Abbey, June 3, 2008.

Matthias Burger

Father Matthias Burger was a contemporary of the monks mentioned above. Born in Idaho into a farming family that moved to Oregon, he made his first profession as a monk of Mount Angel in 1943. A classmate of Fr. Ambrose, he was ordained to the priesthood in 1947 and then sent abroad for studies in Scripture. He had the distinction not only of studying in Rome, but of obtaining an advanced degree from the Pontifical Biblical Institute, the first priest of Mount Angel and the first person in the Northwest to do so.[52] He arrived back at Mount Angel in the early 1950s. Father Matthias con-

Fr. Matthias Burger.

tributed to the community in more than teaching Scripture. He was in charge of abbey landscaping and during the 1950s laid out the signature stone patio in front of the abbey church. He epitomized the "Renaissance monk." He was perhaps the abbey's most noted astronomer, and he built several reflector telescopes and ground his own mirrors. Father Matthias serviced his beloved VW cars and gladly did maintenance for cars of his friends. He relished his time doing sacramental supply to parishes served by Mount Angel, from Alaska to Portland. He also spent a year teaching English at Al Hickma Jesuit University in Baghdad, Iraq, in 1968. After the government closed the school, he came back to embrace the pastoral work of hospital chaplain. He did this for over thirty years in the Portland area, including service as a chaplain to the Legacy Good Samaritan Hospital. Given the breadth of experience and zeal for souls embodied by Fr. Matthias, there is little doubt that his presence on the hilltop in the first years of Abbot Damian's abbatial term helped solidify a strong monastic witness.

52. Necrology of Mount Angel Abbey, July 4, 2001.

CHAPTER FIVE

An Era of Expansion

Post-War Brick and Mortar

BY THE END OF ABBOT DAMIAN'S FIRST DECADE in office, three different but conjoined needs pressed themselves on the community. For the seminary, there was the need to allot adequate physical space to meet the multiple needs of the college and theology departments, along with the day high school. For the community, there was no satisfying venue to offer overnight accommodations to guests and to provide space for retreats. The latter were especially dear to Abbot Damian and he foresaw the urgency of planning for a guest facility. A third projected need was a library that could serve the needs of both the seminary and the monastery. All three of these proposed projects entered the planning and decision-making of the community in the years of Abbot Damian's abbatial tenure.

The most immediate change in the landscape after taking office was the new abbey church. Started under Abbot Thomas, the first decision of significance made by Abbot Damian was both to defer erection of a bell tower and to continue the construction of the monastery's new church. He did that first by completing the excavation for the crypt in 1950 (providing needed space for seminarians and retreatants) and then overseeing the construction of the church in 1951. On the Feast of St. Benedict, March 21, 1952, the new church was consecrated and blessed by Archbishop Howard. It was a testimony to the vision of Abbot Thomas and the detailed determination of Abbot Damian.

July 1951 photo of construction of abbey church crypt and extension.

Aerial view of high school buildings in lower part of picture from 1947.

Blessing of the Abbey Church,
March 21, 1952.

The condition of the high school in the years after the war was not
the best. War-surplus Quonset huts housed the buildings of the school,
and by the mid-1950s these buildings were showing their wear. There
was very limited physical space on the hilltop for new construction.
Spirited discussion within the community on the role of the "Prep Day
School" and its location had taken place.[1] It was decided to look for
new property at the base of Mount Angel's hill. The monastic chapter
ratified the decision in February of 1957 when they agreed to purchase
new land for the high school.[2]

Abbot Damian in 1957 proposed a guest and retreat house that
would provide housing for visitors and also be open for retreats, a
work that Abbot Damian believed was of value to the spiritual witness of the monastery. This proposal was buttressed by the abbot's

1. See the Visitation report of March 3, 1956, Mount Angel Abbey Archives
(hereafter MAAA).

2. Chapter minutes of February 12, 1957. In August of 1959, a new Catholic high
school was opened in the town of Mt. Angel and became coeducational.

long and dedicated commitment to serving as a retreat master for different groups on the hilltop. The most crucial part of the decision to build the guesthouse was its location. For many years the unobstructed view of the valley from the south side of the hilltop was considered sacred. However, by 1957 the community came to see the south end of the monastery as the natural site for the guesthouse. So it was that the monastic chapter on May 20, 1957, gave its approval to build the guesthouse on the southern end of the hilltop.[3] The construction of what became known as Benet Hall began almost two years later in February of 1959 and was not completed until March of 1960; the monastery at last had a designated place for retreats and hospitality. It coincided with a transition in American Benedictine communities from an emphasis on building new educational institutions to one of promoting the apostolate of hospitality.

The new guest facility served to change the character of the monastery in distinct ways. It attracted more of the local clergy for an annual dinner (on March 21) and for priest retreats. Perhaps the most famous of these was one delivered by Bishop Fulton J. Sheen in 1958. Abbot Damian continued to conduct retreats for the Laymen's Guild and Knights of Columbus. Abbot Damian had been in charge of the oblates of the abbey from 1939 to 1951 and sought to incorporate them into the spiritual life of the monastic community. The guesthouse certainly expedited that purpose.

It seemed fitting that one of the first events hosted at the guesthouse was an oblate retreat given by Abbot Damian in July of 1960. For those monks who practiced spiritual direction such as Abbot Damian, Benet Hall offered extra space in a setting outside the monastic cloister. It also brought notable figures to the campus such as the famed American Catholic Church historian Monsignor John Tracy Ellis in 1960. Another distinguished visitor of 1961 was Abbot Leonard Boesch of Engelberg Abbey. It was the first visit of an Engelberg abbot to Mount Angel and heralded a movement toward closer ties in coming years. The guesthouse proved to be a draw for larger Benedictine gatherings. The Swiss-American Congregation General Chapter met at Mount Angel

3. *Abbey Chronicle* LV (1956–60), 6.

Newly completed guesthouse, 1960.

Bishop Fulton J. Sheen giving
a retreat for priests at Mount
Angel, 1958.

in 1962 for the first time in over two decades, thus anticipating related gatherings of Benedictine groups in the following years.

The friendships of Frs. Martin and Luke bore fruit for the wider community on the hilltop in the summer of 1974 when Fr. Jean Leclercq delivered a talk to the summer school of theology. Father Leclercq's visit was followed by one of Fr. Burkhard Neunheuser, a monk of Maria Laach and friend of Fr. Martin, who at that time was the president of the Pontifical Liturgical Institute in Rome. In both of these cases, the monks of Mount Angel benefited from their proximity to the Trappist community of monks at Lafayette, Oregon, where both of these distinguished visitors also spent time.

A New Library and Cultural Outreach

The focus on a new library building and site has its own unique history. There is, first of all, the reality of the destructive character of the fires of 1892 and 1926. These two disasters effectively destroyed most of the abbey and seminary libraries. In the difficult period after the fire of 1926, Mount Angel's European monastic connections once again bore fruit. Through Fr. Maurus Snyder and Fr. Jerome Wespe (the latter at that time was both prior and abbey librarian), the abbeys of Beuron and Maria Laach sent duplicate books to Mount Angel.[4] Then in 1932, Mount Angel received news through St. Matthias Abbey in Trier, Germany, of a "Catholic collection" of books that were to be auctioned in Aachen, Germany. Father Jerome acted quickly, contacting Fr. Martin Pollard in Rome, who had just been ordained. He asked Fr. Martin and his Mount Angel confrere, Frater Luke Eberle, to go to Aachen, inspect the collection, and purchase as much of it as they saw fit. The two young Mount Angel monks worked feverishly to select what they thought would be a representative selection of church history and theology and had it shipped back to Mount Angel in 143 crates in 1933.[5]

Father Mark Schmid succeeded Fr. Jerome as community librarian. What became evident during the decades of the 1930s and '40s was

4. Lawrence McCrank, *Mt. Angel Abbey: A Centennial History of the Benedictine Community and Its Library, 1882–1982* (Wilmington, DE: Scholarly Resources, 1983), 103–4.

5. Fr. Hugh Feiss, OSB, *Mount Angel Abbey Library* booklet (1989).

that Mount Angel fell far short of the quality of neighboring libraries of academic institutions and those of other Benedictine houses. The abbey's first professional librarian was Fr. Barnabas Reasoner. He received his appointment from Abbot Damian when he returned from library school in 1952. Even before that, in the summer of 1947, Frs. Barnabas and Ambrose Zenner visited St. Meinrad Abbey's library and were impressed with what they saw. Led by the efforts of Fr. Barnabas, a Library Committee Report was issued in 1956, along with an evaluation given to community members on a policy of acquisitions and plans for a new library building.[6]

By the 1960s the need for a new library became more pressing. Even as the number of library collections grew, the physical space allotted in Aquinas Hall was totally inadequate to house them. The acute state of cramped quarters pushed the community to heed Abbot Damian's call to construct a new library building. In 1962 Abbot Damian authorized Fr. Barnabas Reasoner to conduct a search for an architect to build a library that would make Mount Angel a cultural center for the region.[7] This was a marked shift from the accustomed architectural selection conforming to utilitarian standards and adherence to a budget. In response to that green light, Fr. Barnabas contacted several noted architects and was pleased to secure for the project one of the famed international architects of that time, Alvar Aalto of Finland. To the surprise of many, Aalto responded positively to the invitation of Fr. Barnabas to serve as chief architect of the library. At a meeting of the abbey chapter held on May 22, 1964, the community voted to build a new library structure. Abbot Damian remarked to the community that the library and the abbey church together with the monastery went hand in hand. A week later the chapter voted to accept Aalto as architect for the library. The famed architect came to Mount Angel in April of 1967 and set in motion plans for a team of associates to do preliminary work for the building. Construction began a year later in May of 1968 and was completed in 1970. A major donor couple, Howard and Jean Vollum of Beaverton, Oregon, spared the community from any prolonged worry about debt incurred in the construction, while

6. Fr. Hugh Feiss, OSB, *Mount Angel Abbey Library* booklet, 116.

7. From a talk given by Emily Horowitz in 1997 to graduate architectural students at the University of Oregon, MAAA.

providing for a necessary endowment that would allow sufficient future maintenance of the facility. Although Aalto never was able to be present for the completion of the structure, he wrote a letter shortly after the dedication that aptly sums up his high estimation of its purpose: "You have personally pressed this building through and it exists because of your intellectual initiative and your personal ambition to have a quality 'instrument' in your hand."[8]

The dedication of the library in May of 1970 brought a notable palette of figures to Mount Angel, from the musical virtuoso Duke Ellington to Abbot Primate Rembert Weakland. Unlike previous history when the library had been regarded as a hidden preserve of the monks and seminarians, it was now seen as being at the center of an apostolate of hospitality for the abbey. It was able to attract a growing number of patrons and cardholders from the region and at the same time provide specialized services through its Center for Patristic and Latin Christian Studies and its Rare Book Collection. The library remained, as Abbot Damian intended, a cultural center for the region and a showpiece for the monastic community and visitors alike. Its collection of over 200,000 volumes of books and special collections served as a beacon for a Benedictine heritage of promotion of learning and intellectual excellence.

Another cultural landmark that was established in the time of Abbot Damian was the summer Bach Festival. This was an attempt to use the unique ambience of the hilltop as a place to invite internationally recognized musical artists to offer musical performances over several days in July, using the abbey church, the library, other facilities, and the beauty of the lawn for al fresco dining. Mrs. Michel McKay was instrumental in promoting the Bach Festival as executive director in its early years, and it became a cultural highlight of the summer in the Willamette Valley. It tapped into the long tradition of musical appreciation and performance associated with the monastery. It also utilized the Foyer Gallery of the new library as an exhibit space and the larger mezzanine as a venue for performance and a site to showcase the monastery's artistic outreach. The Bach Festival established a connection with segments of the unchurched and artistic circles of

8. Horowitz, 2.

Aerial view of the Aalto Library, 1970.

Abbot Damian on the lawn with visitors for the first Bach Festival, 1972.

surrounding society that prior to the festival had made little contact with the monastery. The Bach Festival continues as a vibrant cultural symbol of Mount Angel to this day.

The Seminary

Whereas such ventures as the Benet Hall Guesthouse, the Aalto Library and the Bach Festival were initiated and promoted by Abbot Damian, the status of the seminary in the years of Abbot Damian's tenure was more complex and problematic. Given the place it occupied as the central apostolic work of the community and the fluctuating fortunes of seminaries throughout the decades of the 1960s and '70s, Mount Angel Seminary merited renewed attention.

The relationship that Abbot Damian had with the seminary was an intimate one. In the course of his time at Mount Angel he had been rector, dean, and professor of moral theology. He believed that the task of seminary education was an essential aspect of the mission of the abbey and needed to be preserved and promoted.

As noted earlier, the separation of the college from the seminary that was made definitive by Abbot Thomas in 1946 began a period of change for Mount Angel's educational apostolate. This allowed a more uniform and monastic environment to take root within all twelve years of the seminary program operating at the time. This monastic character of the schools was reinforced by the fact that only Benedictine monks from the abbey served as rectors and until 1967 the abbot of Mount Angel retained the title of president of Mount Angel Seminary. Moreover, Mount Angel Seminary existed in these years not as a separate corporate entity but as part of a larger Mount Angel corporation sole.

The enrollment of the seminary student body continued to grow through the decade of the 1950s and early 1960s. There were separate rectors in place for both the minor seminary (which at that time included four years of high school and two of college) and the major seminary (that included two years of college and four of theology). Greater screening and testing were now in place for incoming students, as well as a "pastoral" fifth year of theology. The appearance of lay faculty members signaled another adjustment from previous all clerical instructors.

A change that was of significance took place in February of 1964 when the Archdiocese of Portland announced that it had purchased the Mount Angel High School from the abbey, thus putting an end to the day school in town. Other changes aggravated planning for seminary enrollment. The "Normal School" in Mt. Angel operated by the Benedictine sisters went coeducational in the late 1950s. In 1964 the sisters made a request of the monastery to change their name to Mount Angel College, since that title had been dropped at the seminary in 1947. That change notwithstanding, by the mid-1960s the sisters' college was to close its doors.

1964 also coincided with the seventy-fifth anniversary of the seminary. To celebrate that milestone there was an impressive gathering at Mount Angel on May 13. Cardinal James McIntyre of Los Angeles was present, as was Archbishop Howard. It was to be one of the last events at which Archbishop Howard presided as ordinary. Beneath this celebratory veneer, however, there were disturbing changes for the seminary's future. The archdiocese, on the suggestion of a committee appointed by Archbishop Howard, laid plans for a "house of studies" for its college-age seminarians at Portland State University.[9] This house did open in 1968, and it was to siphon the major flow of archdiocesan and regional seminarians away from Mount Angel for almost two decades. This coincided with a push by Archbishop Thomas Connolly of Seattle to have bishops of the Northwest make St. Thomas Theological Seminary in Seattle their regional major seminary, putting in jeopardy another major source of seminary students for Mount Angel.

All of this required a response on the part of Abbot Damian and the monastic community. In fall of 1967, a new administrative structure for the seminary was put in place. There would now be a threefold division of high school, college, and theology, each including a four-year program of study and each having its own rector. The abbot retained the position of chancellor and there were three Benedictine rectors. Two years later, Abbot Damian appointed a Chancellor's Committee to review avenues of how the entire seminary structure could best be reprogrammed to deal with the unprecedented set of circumstances

9. Fr. Martin Pollard, ed., *Fratribus Nostris Absentibus* 172 (November 1966), MAAA.

confronting the seminary. The committee came to the conclusion that the 1967 organizational change had resulted in needless duplication of administrative functions and poor utilization of human resources.[10] The principal recommendation that came from this report was to create the post of president rector, a person who would coordinate the administrative duties of the theology, college, and high school seminary. The chancellor would still retain authority over the president rector, but there was to be an autonomy that would sever the strict monastic control that had been exercised previously. The result was that in May of 1969 Abbot Damian announced that Fr. Boniface Lautz would become the president rector and in that position be charged with overseeing the three main divisions of the seminary, four years of theology, four of the college seminary, and four in the minor seminary. Abbot Damian, as chancellor, and Fr. Boniface, as president rector, then established a Board of Regents, composed of the bishops and vocation directors who sent seminarians to Mount Angel.

All of these players were to be caught up in the theological renewal that was part and parcel of the change that affected other areas of the hilltop in the 1960s. The climate of change or what some deemed the culture of unrest was at work in the local Catholic church as well. The competing entities for seminary education being implemented by the archdioceses of Portland and Seattle required some adjustment on the part of Mount Angel.[11] Along with these competing challenges, there occurred the marked decline in numbers of seminarians after the Second Vatican Council. In the face of all this, Mount Angel recognized the need to collaborate more with fellow educators in the Northwest to meet the ever-changing character of seminary education in what was unchartered territory.

The one constant thread apparent in the changed structure of the seminary through the 1960s and '70s was that the control exercised by the monks lessened with each succeeding year. Removing the abbot from the administrative leadership and having diocesan priests serve as rectors became indices of this change. Yet through it all Mount

---

10. Chancellor's Committee Report of May 5, 1969, MAAA.

11. As the experiments of the House of Studies at Portland State and St. Thomas Seminary in Seattle played out, they both closed their doors in the 1970s.

Angel's seminary managed to preserve a reputation of adhering to authentic church teaching and adapting well to the pastoral needs of a post-Vatican II church.

New Foundations

Two new requests came to the Mount Angel community in the early 1960s. One was from the bishop of Cuernavaca, Mexico, Sergio Mendez Arceo. He requested to have a Benedictine community attached to his minor seminary. Bishop Mendez Arceo had visited Mount Angel and thought that the monks were a good fit for this project. It was also exquisite timing on his part, for this request came just after Pope Pius XII and Pope John XXIII had exhorted religious communities of men in North America to consider sending 10 percent of their personnel to provide assistance to the needs of the Church in Latin America. A chapter meeting was held on December 22, 1964, and the monks of Mount Angel voted to make a foundation in Mexico.

On August 12 of the following year, Fr. Ambrose Zenner was called to Abbot Damian's office and told that he was to be entrusted with the enterprise of heading the foundation in the Diocese of Cuernavaca and possibly starting a major seminary for the diocese. He would leave within ten days to begin language study in Mexico. This all came as an absolute surprise to Fr. Ambrose. Nonetheless, he accepted the appointment to be the superior of the monastic foundation.[12] He knew how his gift of learning foreign languages would serve him well in this role, and he also relished the challenge of heading a new monastic foundation.

Father Ambrose spent his first few months in Mexico in 1965 at Monsignor Ivan Illich's Center for Intercultural Formation. Part of his formation was to learn the language and culture and make contacts with a variety of other missionaries. He also took time to write an ongoing "Report from Mexico" for the Mount Angel community that is rich in detail and observation of his experience.[13] Upon his arrival

12. Fr. Augustine DeNoble, OSB "Anniversary and History," *Monasterio Benedictino Nuestra Senora de Los Angeles Newsletter* 13, no. 1 (May 1983), 1.

13. See the September 4, October 10, and November 20, 1965 letters, MAAA.

in Mexico, Fr. Ambrose made contact with Prior Odo Zimmermann of the St. John's Abbey Community in Mexico City and Mother Mildred Knoebber of the Atchison, Kansas, community of Benedictine women, along with a network of other missionaries. Their advice and friendship were to be valuable assets in the upcoming years.

One of the more controversial aspects of Mount Angel's move to Cuernavaca was over another monastic community located there. The Monastery of St. Mary of the Resurrection had been in operation for some years when Mount Angel sent its first monks to Cuernavaca in 1965. It was at this time that the Resurrection Monastery was attracting attention and some negative impressions. This was largely due to a controversial use of psychoanalysis under the direction of its prior, Fr. Gregory Lemercier. Even though Bishop Mendez Arceo was aware of this and gave it his approval, it created consternation in the Benedictine world (two special visitations of the Abbot Primate were made in 1963 and 1964).[14] Father Ambrose did his best to distance the Mount Angel foundation from that of Fr. Lemercier's.

Another figure of controversy in Cuernavaca was Monsignor Illich. A number of articles of his roundly criticizing American missionaries in Central America became a cause of concern, especially when it was learned that Monsignor Illich was in charge of the program at the Center for Intercultural Formation that Fr. Ambrose was part of in Cuernavaca during the summer of 1965. To the credit of Fr. Ambrose, he kept his distance from the provocative comments emanating from the center, and there was no discernible influence that Monsignor Illich had on the monastic vision of the Mount Angel Mexican Priory.

Father Ambrose finished his classes at the center in November of 1965 and was joined shortly after by Br. Boniface Archederra, a monk of Mount Angel who had lived for thirty-three years in Mexico before entering the community, and thus he was well acclimated to both the language and the culture in Cuernavaca. Father Ambrose and Br. Boniface were joined by Abbot Damian, who arrived in Mexico City on December 17, and over the following days had extensive conversations with Bishop Mendez Arceo and some of his priests. The upshot

14. Two members of this monastery joined the Mount Angel monks in Cuernavaca in June of 1967.

Photo of first community of monks in Cuernavaca.

of this meeting was that Mount Angel agreed to assume for three years responsibility of the minor seminary for the Diocese of Cuernavaca and other surrounding dioceses, with Fr. Ambrose as rector. This proposal was brought before the Mount Angel chapter on January 2, 1966, and approved.[15] Once again, the apostolate of seminary education was at the center of Mount Angel's corporate presence.

Father Bruno Becker arrived from Mount Angel in February of 1966. After finishing his studies at the Center for Intercultural Documentation Formation Center in June, he was given jobs of publicity and fundraising for the priory, while Br. Boniface was in charge of all the finances of the priory and seminary. On August 15, 1966, Abbot Damian came to the cathedral in Cuernavaca to celebrate a pontifical Mass with Bishop Mendez Arceo. Father Ambrose, Fr. Bruno, and Br. Boniface joined them. At this event, the priory was formally erected and given its name: The Monastery of Our Lady of the Angels. At the same ceremony a cornerstone was blessed for what would be the future site of the monastery. That locale began its development in 1967 at a tract of land called Ahuatepec outside of the city. With the help of Fr. Dominic Broxmeyer, the farm boss from

15. Chapter minutes, January 2, 1966.

Mount Angel who came down for a visit, recommendations were made on how to best develop the land. The community moved from their place in the city to the new monastery in September of 1967.

Father Ambrose went to great pains to both maintain a strong educational presence at the seminary and nurture a monastic climate at the priory. The community began praying a full and restructured Divine Office in Spanish by November of 1967. In the next years the buildings housing the monastery and the seminary were remodeled. Twelve rooms were built to house the monks and twenty double rooms were constructed to house the seminary. The monks also drew from the example of Fr. Alcuin Heibel's rural community in the 1940s and formed farm co-ops in the area to improve the life of a largely agricultural community surrounding them. On February 2, 1968, the first unit of the new monastery was blessed and dedicated by Bishop Mendez Arceo and Abbot Damian.

On December 22, 1964, at the same chapter meeting where the monks of Mount Angel agreed to make their Mexico foundation, they gave an affirmative reply to a request that had been made by Bishop Treinen of Boise, Idaho, asking for monks of Mount Angel to make a foundation in his diocese. In some fashion, this was a return of monks to Idaho from the time when Abbot Frowin Conrad, in 1904, had labored to found a monastic community from Conception Abbey in Cottonwood, Idaho.[16] The bishop offered 600 acres of semi-desert land that he and a priest of his diocese, Fr. Nicholas Walsh, had secured from the federal government. The former bishop of Idaho, James Byrne, had visited Mount Angel in 1958. At that time, he petitioned Abbot Damian to establish a Catholic high school in Idaho, much as the earlier community in Cottonwood from Conception had done.[17] The chapter of Mount Angel, however, rejected the proposal.

For Abbot Damian, who had spent his youth in Idaho, there was enthusiasm when Bishop Treinen returned in 1964 with an offer that included

16. That community, Mount Saint Michael, was forced to close in 1924, although Benedictine sisters of the Monastery of St. Gertrude kept a Benedictine presence in Idaho from 1907 to the present.

17. John O'Hagan, *Monastery of the Ascension, 1965–2015* (private printing, 2016), 19.

The first Mass on the Idaho Priory property is celebrated at an outdoor altar by Bishop Sylvester Treinen, with Prior Patrick Meagher, Abbot Damian, and Fr. Nicholas Walsh, August 3, 1965.

the gift of land and the hope of a future seminary for the training of young men for the priesthood, a work closely connected to Mount Angel. Optimism was generated about making the only male Benedictine monastery in the state and certainly contributed to the motive of the chapter to give approval to the project. In February of 1965 Fr. Patrick Meagher was sent to explore the land and its possibilities. Supported by Fr. Nicholas Walsh, a friend and benefactor of the abbey (and later bishop), the land near Jerome, Idaho, was deeded to the abbey in May and in July Fr. Patrick was appointed as the first prior of the new Idaho foundation. Four monks were sent to Idaho, and on August 3 Mass was celebrated outdoors on the future monastery's property. The initial expectation of Bishop Treinen to have Mount Angel monks conduct a seminary was put on hold. Instead, the bishop offered the community property owned by the diocese just off the campus of the College of Southern Idaho in Twin Falls. He proposed that the monks staff a Catholic student center there. By that time Fr. Patrick was joined by Fr. Simeon Van de Voord from Mount Angel. Ground was broken in October of 1968, and in June of 1969 the Idaho monks had their first real home in the St. Benedict's Student Center and Priory of Twin Falls. It was to be their home until 1980. In those years the work with the students and other programs such as Marriage Encounter and pre-Cana solidified the sentiment against starting a seminary.

The completed Ascension monastery from the air, Jerome, Idaho.

Meanwhile the monks of Westminster Abbey in British Columbia had forged ahead with their development. In 1944 Fr. Cyril Leibold returned to Mount Angel and was replaced as prior by Fr. Eugene Medved. In that same year Fr. Luke Eberle came to Canada as rector of the seminary. In June of 1948 the Canada community became a conventual priory, and a year later the major and minor seminary were assigned in perpetuity to the monks of Westminster. In 1953 the community became an abbey, and Eugene Medved was elected as the first abbot. A gracious gesture on the part of Mount Angel was the promise of providing free education for all of the monks of Westminster at Mount Angel's seminary if it were the choice of the Canadian community. The next year witnessed a significant move of the Westminster monks to Mission, British Columbia. It was a relocation that afforded more space for both the seminary and monastery. In the decades of the 1950s and '60s that space was filled with seminary structures, a barn, and a guesthouse. In many respects the Westminster foundation carried the genetic package of its mother-house. The monks treasured the beauty of a "high ground" location and the responsibility of providing quality seminary education. They made land purchases that guaranteed financial stability, allowed the opportunity to have a sustainable agricultural presence in the community, and assured room to expand in the future. The spiritual life and leadership of the community in its pioneer stages displayed in multiple details the tradition of Mount Angel.

Dealing with Church Renewal

Along with many other Catholic institutions and Benedictine communities, the monks of Mount Angel confronted the challenge of dealing with the forces of renewal in the church and the unprecedented currents of societal upheaval that were so closely identified with the decade of the 1960s.

In one respect, the mission of Mount Angel seemed secure as the decade began. The community's educational apostolates from the high school through the School of Theology gave evidence of growth in numbers and administrative efficiency. The widespread presence of Mount Angel priest-monks in the pastoral care of countless parishes in the Portland archdiocese and beyond was seen as a given. The physical expansion of buildings on the hilltop underscored the optimism that was a hallmark of the wider Catholic Church of that era. The community's increase in numbers was a sufficient index for many of the fact that generations of hard work had borne fruit. The two new foundations in Mexico and Idaho were yet another indication of the positive outlook that was mirrored by the monks of Mount Angel.

At the same time, there were indicators of concern surrounding the impressive infrastructure of monastic personnel and physical expansion. A recurring criticism heard within the community and articulated in visitation reports during these years was of overworked monks.[18] This extended from people in administrative positions to those who were part of the still considerable manual labor force of the institution.

There was also concern over the continuance of both the *St. Josephs Blatt* and *St. Joseph Magazine,* both of which were down to low subscription levels and losing money. Some of the tensions that had been masked in the flush of the first decade of Abbot Damian's physical expansion and support of a vigorous monastic community life now began to manifest themselves.

18. See Abbot Stephen Schappler, *Recessus* of the Visitation of February 28–March 3, 1956, Swiss-American Congregational Archives (hereafter SACA).

Tensions Within

One of the reliable barometers of community consensus and morale was the regular canonical visitation. This involved a periodic visit by monks from outside the home abbey to interview community members and assess the spiritual and temporal health of the community. The decade of the 1960s saw several of these visitations and the reports reflect the tensions and calls for change that were so much a part of these years, both in the church and in the wider world.

One area of contention within the Mount Angel community in these years was over leadership. In 1965 and 1966, a number of Mount Angel monks had signed petitions addressed to Abbot Damian, calling for changes within the house. When these did not produce any discernible response on the part of the abbot, petitioners wrote to the abbot president of the Swiss-American Congregation, David Melancon. In a letter to Abbot Damian in late 1966, Abbot David recounted in some detail the comments he had received from Mount Angel community members critical of his leadership.[19]

There was a subsequent visitation made to Mount Angel by Abbot David in March of 1968. At that visitation a recommendation was made to Abbot Damian "to resign [as abbot] for his peace and wellbeing as well as that of the community."[20] This recommendation came as a jarring surprise for a spiritual leader of the monastic community who had been under the impression that he was a stabilizing force in a sea of uncertainty.

In July of that same year Abbot Damian gave a rejoinder to Abbot David that capsulized much of his reluctance to support the impulse for change within the monastic community: "I wonder whether as superiors we are not at fault by being too permissive in renewal, thinking it to be renewal when it is not renewal at all but rather giving in to too much fancy in so-called updating. In reality it is permitting liberty to destroy true service of God in a life dedicated to Him."[21]

19. Letter of Abbot David Melancon to Abbot Damian, November 4, 1966, SACA.

20. Visitation report, SACA.

21. Letter of Abbot Damian to Abbot David Melancon, July 30, 1968, SACA.

Nonetheless, there were some efforts on Abbot Damian's part to introduce change for some customary practices. In September of 1968 the title "Frater" was dropped, and all non-ordained monks were to be called "Brother." In March of 1969, a buffet supper without table reading on Sunday evening was introduced. In April of that same year, the chapter voted to admit brothers to full membership in the community.[22] In January of 1970, the Abbey Council was enlarged to six members, with three now being elected by the community.

The liturgical change to the vernacular from the Latin was possibly the most profound change that took place. The 1960s was truly a watershed for this introduction of English into the Mass and Divine Office. One can trace the movement of the change with the approval of the Constitution on the Sacred Liturgy by the Second Vatican Council in 1964. The first Mass in English was on the feast of Martin of Tours, November 11, 1964.[23] This coincided with the installation of a second altar in the sanctuary that allowed the celebrant to face the people. The Chapter of Faults or Culpa Chapter was changed from Latin to English on December 4, 1964. The mealtime prayers were recited in English for the first time on April 18, 1965 (Easter Sunday), and the Martyrology, now moved to the conclusion of the midday meal in the refectory, began the use of English on June 20, 1965. The first use of English in the Divine Office was at Compline, during the first week of June in 1967. This was also the date when the lay brothers joined in the prayer of Compline. Finally, all of the Office hours were prayed in English from January 3, 1968 on.

Abbot Damian supported most of these changes, especially as they helped to unify the community. He wrote in 1968: "The principal advantage of our experimental office is that it has made possible the unification of our community, lay brothers with priest monks and clerics, in our public worship."[24] A new Solesmes method of chant was adopted as Fr. David Nicholson was appointed choirmaster. It was in

22. The first brothers who took solemn vows did so on September 6, 1969, becoming full-fledged members of the community chapter.

23. July 7, 2017 interview with Fr. Augustine DeNoble.

24. Report submitted by Abbot Damian and Liturgy Subcommittee to Cardinal Benno Gut, May 14, 1968, MAAA.

the demands made by some for changes in the music that would reflect the vernacular that prompted Abbot Damian to emphasize caution, if not reticence, in the consideration of any alteration of traditional practices. A letter he wrote to Archbishop Dwyer of Portland reflected this attitude: "In the present effort [to] renewal, anytime anything is said or done to stabilize or to slow down the mad rush of change, to halt the race seeking little beside greater liberty, you meet the opposite of indifference."[25] In retrospect, one notes the labored effort of Abbot Damian to preserve what was best in the community's liturgical tradition and not abandon all customary practices. The respectable intentions of Abbot Damian in the matter of liturgical adaptation did not always square with the impression that others perceived. Abbot Damian's initial reluctance to concelebrate at the conventual Mass was one possible example of this.

If there remains a valid criticism of Abbot Damian in these years, it is not that he saw the wider sweep of church renewal in a negative light. In his position as religious superior he was involved in most of the major monastic meetings that dealt with renewal, including the Abbots' Congress in Rome in 1967 and the General Chapters of the Congregation in 1968 and 1969. Abbot Damian found it difficult, however, to involve segments of the wider community in the renewal process, and that is at the heart of the heaviest criticism he received from his confreres. As one monk wrote in a letter to the abbot president in 1969: "Policy belongs to the abbot alone; he makes it and keeps it."[26]

Abbot David Melancon attempted to have Abbot Damian see the need for this when he wrote to him: "I would certainly appreciate knowing what it is you are referring to when you write that 'what we are doing is not renewal and not Vatican II.' I assume that in many things not all of us will agree, but I am definitely interested in having each one's view expressed and considered. It seems to me that only in this way can we come to the best possible decisions about what is good and right and desirable."[27]

25. Letter of Abbot Damian to Archbishop Robert Dwyer, February 15, 1969, MAAA.

26. Letter of Fr. Blaise Turck to Abbot David Melancon, February 24, 1969, SACA.

27. Letter of Abbot David Melancon to Abbot Damian, August 1, 1968, SACA.

While Abbot Damian did not relish the delegation of authority, he saw himself as a safeguard for the monastic community against intemperate change that he felt was being rushed. This feeling is made clear in words he wrote in the *Mount Angel Letter* of June 1970: "At times we have the impression that we are moving so fast that we are unable to guide the horse or the car and it is just a question of how long before a smash-up will result."[28]

There were also enterprises outside of the internal monastic renewal that were vexing Abbot Damian. One of these was an ambitious building project that in retrospect seemed to embody much of the overweaning ambitions of the day.

In the late 1950s Father Hildebrand Melchior of the Mount Angel community initiated a project in concert with a number of businessmen in the town of Mt. Angel. It was to be a Catholic retirement complex of cottages, with its own chapel and resident chaplain and a capacity of over 400 persons. It was a proposal visionary in every sense, far ahead of its time with regard to making provisions for the elderly. In December of 1960 fifteen acres of abbey land was sold to "Angel Towers," and in June of 1961 the Mount Angel Towers Project was announced in the *Mount Angel Letter*.[29] In 1962 the Mount Angel chapter agreed "to lend its moral support to preserving the Towers corporation in existence, and to conduct fund-raising drives within the dignity of Mount Angel Abbey and of the Church, the proceeds of which will be made available to the mortgage or corporation."[30] By 1963 the plan had evolved to a six-story building of over two hundred units, to be built at the eastern edge of the town at the foot of the hilltop, on land formerly owned by the abbey. In 1963 senior citizens were invited to make deposits for their residences, and a substantial loan for the project was secured through the Federal Housing Administration. Construction costs soared far beyond expectations, to over $3 million. By the end of 1965 residents were able to move in. Shortly after, Fr. Hildebrand took up residence as chaplain, and the units were occupied. Within a short time, it became evident that the project's financial viability was in jeopardy, and they faced bankruptcy. In March of 1967 the Federal Housing Authority

28. *Mount Angel Letter* (June 1970), 8.
29. *Mount Angel Letter* (June 1961), 4.
30. Chapter minutes of December 15, 1962.

took over the building and put it into federal receivership. In September of that same year a sizeable number of residents wrote to the local FHA head, Oscar Pederson, with a list of complaints centered on the role of Fr. Hildebrand.[31] Archbishop Robert Dwyer was made aware of the potential scandal for the church in the matter, and, with the acquiescence of Abbot Damian, sent a number of officials from the archdiocese to investigate. Their report, delivered to the archbishop in March of 1968, was critical of Fr. Hildebrand's role in the Towers Project on several accounts.[32] In June of 1968 the Towers was sold to the FHA. In 1969 the Evangelical Lutheran Good Samaritan Society took over the Towers. Under its new management, the Towers had full occupancy by 1972. It was purchased from the government by Gene and Irene Fenton, and under the subsequent direction of Sr. Louise Olberding it operated efficiently.[33]

The ensuing cloud of suspicion over mismanagement of the project was directed at the abbey. Abbot Damian responded to criticism in a 1964 *Mount Angel Letter:* "The abbey is not a member of the corporate building, the Towers, even though the corporation was made up of individuals of Mount Angel and neighboring communities. The abbey has nothing to do with financing of the project."[34] Despite the disclaimers of Abbot Damian, there was a feeling on the part of the monastic chapter that he had been disingenuous about the role of Fr. Hildebrand in the project and had failed to communicate the implications of the bankruptcy to the community. The members of the abbey also felt that the trust of the community on the part of the local population was undermined. This became another factor that had monks question the abbatial mode of leadership.

In fact, the Towers scandal was only one of a series of critical conditions that faced the community in the decade of the 1960s. *St. Joseph Magazine* and the *St. Josephs Blatt* were losing money at the Press and

---

31. Letter of Tower residents to Oscar Pedersen, September 2, 1967, MAAA.

32. Report to Archbishop Dwyer from six representatives of the archdiocese, March 5, 1968, MAAA.

33. *Oregon Statesman*, Salem (January 14, 1977), 17. It was revealing that in 1973 the Abbey Chapter turned down an offer to purchase the Towers.

34. *Mount Angel Letter* (September 1964), 4.

many questioned the prudence of their continued publication.[35] The high school seminary remained a bone of contention with respect to its physical location and effectiveness. Furthermore, its administrative functioning was complicated with the previously mentioned restructuring of the seminary that began in 1967. The financial and managerial status of the farm operation was in fragile shape. Fires in the hog barns in 1955 and the beef barn in 1961 required major new investments and now declining revenues and diminishing monastic workers added to its problematic future.

There was also an understandable concern about the physical health of Abbot Damian. Many thought the abbot was insensitive to complaints of overwork on the part of the monks because their leader was burdened by too many tasks. They included a daunting list of retreats given each year, the role of chaplain to the Benedictine sisters, and his position as president of the seminary, to say nothing of the many people for whom he offered spiritual direction.

An added concern surfaced in January of 1967 when Abbot Damian was diagnosed with diabetes. This condition was later aggravated by a bad case of shingles in 1971 that developed into Bell's palsy. In the latter case he went to the hospital only after being "ordered" by his prior, Fr. Anselm Galvin, after several days of gamely going to Divine Office while in much distress.

The skepticism Abbot Damian retained with respect to renewal in the wider ecclesial and monastic worlds deepened in the last years of his life. This may have been a factor in his seeming imperviousness to listen and to understand what some of those pressing for change in the Mount Angel community wanted. The strong sense of duty in his position as abbot, along with a surety of conscience that he knew best the direction and the pace of renewal for the community blunted any possibility of a more collaborative effort of decision making.

Abbot Damian remained resolute in representing the community at key renewal meetings. That included his presence at the extraordinary General Chapter at St. Joseph's Abbey in Louisiana in the fall of 1969.

---

35. The abbey chapter voted to sell *St. Josephs Blatt* in 1966. The last issue printed by Mount Angel Abbey was December 30, 1966. It had been in operation for seventy years. *Saint Joseph Magazine* published its last issue in July 1968.

It was at this meeting that the Swiss-American Congregation approved its Declaration on Monastic Life and new constitution. On a local level, Abbot Damian was asked to organize the religious superiors of the Northwest in 1971 to help expedite renewal efforts, a sign of the esteem he had among his peers in consecrated life.

It should be noted that there were Mount Angel monks who were also in the forefront of the broader renewal of monastic life. Father Martin Pollard had been involved in preparation for the revision of the "Declarations on the Rule and Constitutions" in the mid-1960s. Father Blaise Turck was a secretary to the General Chapter of 1969 and played a role in drafting the initial version of the *Covenant of Peace* declaration of 1969. Father Thomas Brockhaus was the elected community delegate to the General Chapter of 1969 and served as a canonical consultant for the Swiss-American Congregation.

Nonetheless, there was still a gulf between the direction that was given from the abbot's position as superior of the community and the professed members. This was made evident in the community visitation of 1971. At that time, deep tensions and rifts were named by the visitors. There was a recommendation for more consultation with the community and better communication of information. A pressing issue that surfaced at the visitation was the lay brothers expression of the wish that they should be more fully integrated into the community.[36] Although Abbot Damian had some misgivings about the readiness of the lay brothers to be more deeply integrated into the monastic life, it took place by increments from 1969 to 1973. Given all of the questionable adaptations that took place in the renewal period after Vatican II, the incorporation of the brothers into the abbey with full chapter rights and into the monastic choir proved to be a positive and significant landmark in the life of the community.

A recurring critique made of Abbot Damian in his later years as abbot was that he failed to sense how great a gulf there was between his thinking and that of his monastic community. On his part, Abbot Damian believed it was essential to preserve monastic practices and a reverence for the Catholic and Benedictine character of Mount Angel that he thought was jeopardized by what he saw as the overly insis-

36. Visitation report of 1971, MAAA.

tent demand for change. A case can be made that there was, if not a silent majority, a substantial part of the community that shared the perspective of Abbot Damian. The fact that they were less vocal and uncertain about how best to articulate that perspective only added to the community unease.

It helps to understand the situation at Mount Angel between 1964 and 1974 within the wider ecclesial world. During this time discordant notes of distrust of authority and complaints about the slow pace of change emanated from the pews of the faithful, as well as the choir stalls of monks. Mount Angel was certainly not alone in having its tensions and internal debate on what exactly renewal meant. In tandem with other communities at the time, these tensions inevitably became part of its public persona.

Abbot Damian's health continued to decline in the 1970s, but it was only in the summer of 1974 that he was diagnosed with cancer and had to leave the monastery and take up residence in medical care facilities. Abbot Damian's intention was to preside at monastic professions in September and then step down from office. His cancer's rapid spread, however, did not allow for that to happen. He died in the hospital on September 1, 1974, the first Mount Angel abbot to die while in office.

At the funeral liturgy for Abbot Damian on September 5, 1974, Archbishop Robert Dwyer, a kindred spirit to the superior, aptly summarized Abbot Damian's legacy in words of his eulogy:

> He insisted on a reasonably ordered transition and the presentation of a sense of the sacred in the liturgy. If he wept inwardly at what was inferior if not banal, he hid his tears. In comparison with many other Benedictine houses similarly affected, Mount Angel, under his rule, came off well and holds the promise of genuine renewal.[37]

Archbishop Dwyer captured a monastic ethos of Abbot Damian that not all of his contemporary religious superiors had—a singular dedication to slow and measured adaptation, and an abhorrence of whatever detracted from the sacred in worship.

What is beyond question is that the period of Abbot Damian's abbatial tenure was the longest in the history of Mount Angel. It encompassed a

---

37. *Mount Angel Letter* (October 1974), 3.

period of growth and change that was unprecedented. He was clearly the main force behind the building of the new guesthouse and library, both of which were bold moves for the time and helped to have a much wider circle of people come to know and respect Mount Angel and its monastic character. Many of his contemporaries would have credited him as an exemplar of the monks of his generation: a man of deep spiritual commitment and values, hardworking and zealous for the well-being of Benedictine life and his beloved community of Mount Angel. His shadow looms large over the corporate memory of the monastery.

CHAPTER SIX

Changed Directions in Leadership and Work

Shifting Elements

T HE PERSON WHO SERVED AS PRIOR for Abbot Damian in his last three years, Fr. Anselm Galvin, was another monk whose broad range of assignments over the years gave him a familiarity with the community mission. He had come to know the work of the Press when serving for twelve years as associate editor of *St. Joseph Magazine.* He was familiar with the entire spectrum of monastic formation by dint of serving as novice master under Abbot Thomas and brother master under Abbot Damian. In the monastery's educational apostolate, he was a seminary professor for twenty years and had an administrative role as principal of the seminary high school from 1967 to 1972.[1] In his role as prior from 1971 to 1974, he had the opportunity to be privy to all of the major issues that were being faced by the community. His performance of duty as prior seemed to win the confidence of many of the community members, since he was chosen as abbot when the community met for the election on October 8, 1974. That confidence and support were reflected in the presence of three archbishops of Portland present at his November 26 blessing: Archbishop Cornelius Power who presided at the liturgy and retired Archbishops Howard

---

1. Necrology of January 11, 1994.

and Dwyer. Noteworthy, too, was the participation of Abbot Leonard from Engelberg, a supportive presence from the motherhouse.

Abbot Anselm felt the weight of the many challenges facing the community at this juncture in their history. The two dependent foundations in Idaho and Mexico were in the midst of redefining themselves. The Monastery of the Ascension in Idaho moved over the course of two years (1978–80) from Twin Falls to the original acreage in Jerome. The original idea of building and staffing a seminary was no longer part of the priory's mission. It became incumbent on the Idaho priory to choose a work and a monastic identity that fit the needs of their new place and time.

The Cuernavaca community faced a leadership transition. Father Ambrose Zenner, the founding superior of the community, was reassigned to parish work in Oregon in 1975.[2] The Mexican community had to cope with the task of developing new leadership and changing their principal apostolate from seminary education to hospitality.[3] The seminary was converted into a guest wing and the new monastery in Ahuatepec was in the final stages of construction.

Another arena where Abbot Anselm was required to show attention was the seminary. In the early 1970s there was a notable drop in enrollment, particularly in the high school seminary and the college. This coincided with a tumultuous current of student demand for change, a phenomenon not unique to Mount Angel. In the early 1970s, the School of Theology was in competition with St. Thomas Seminary in Seattle for diocesan seminarians of the Northwest. In response to this the Board of Regents and the Mount Angel Chapter embarked on a new educational enterprise, initiating a summer school course of philosophical and theological studies to qualified women religious.[4] The Summer School of Theology began operation in 1973 and brought in 180–200 students in its first years. It helped to compensate for the declining student population in the seminary. In 1978 a Hispanic Ministry Program was initiated, anticipating the outreach that would

2. Father Ambrose met with a tragic death as a result of an auto accident shortly after his return to Oregon on May 2, 1976.

3. The Seminary at Cuernavaca was closed in 1974.

4. Within two years this would be expanded to lay men and women.

Blessing of Abbot Anselm Galvin by Archbishop Cornelius Power,
November 26, 1974.

be required pastorally to deal with the burgeoning Spanish-speaking
population in the Northwest in decades ahead.

   A group of young monastic administrators, originally appointed by
Abbot Damian to oversee these changes, had their hands full. The cultural turbulence of the late 1960s required all of the skills of adaptation
and firmness of purpose that the monastic administration could mus-
ter. Fathers Bernard Sander, Boniface Lautz, Edmund Smith, Andrew
Baumgartner, Gregory Duerr, and Hugh Feiss all held administrative
positions in the years of transition from the 1960s to the 1970s. Their
experience told them that there needed to be a broadened base of administration and governance. So it was that a Board of Trustees was
established (to supplement the previous Board of Regents of Bishops),
as well as an openness to non-Benedictines in the position of rector.[5]

   5. Much of this history can be found in an oral set of interviews with former
seminary administrators organized by Fr. Nathan Zodrow (private transcript from
March 18, 1997, meeting in the Mount Angel Guesthouse).

It was eventually decided to appoint a diocesan priest, Fr. Elden Curtiss, as rector of the School of Theology in 1972, the first non-Benedictine to hold the post. This set the precedent for successive appointments of diocesan priests in the position as rector. Moreover, Abbot Anselm no longer served in the position of president of the seminary.

While there was much flux occurring for the major seminary, the community's high school seminary had its last commencement on May 26, 1979, closing its doors afterward. Dwindling enrollment, the difficulty of finding adequate personnel to staff the school, and budget deficits all contributed to the community decision. Mount Angel knew it was not alone in shuttering the doors of part of its seminary. St. Meinrad Archabbey had closed its high school minor seminary in 1966 and Conception Abbey eliminated its School of Theology in the 1970s, attesting to how such closures were "signs of the times."

Another traditional enterprise of the monastery that faced change at this time was the abbey farm. For years the farm had been under the administration of the monks and had supplied considerable amounts of fresh food for the kitchens of the monastery and schools. Changing tax laws and budgetary imbalances required that in 1975 the monastery would face the prospect of leasing its farmland for others to manage if it were to survive. On October 28, 1975, the monastic chapter agreed to do just that.[6] On November 4, the abbey hop operations and remaining farmland were leased, and before the end of the calendar year the forest land and its timber were outsourced, and the dairy herd was sold.[7] The Milk Ranch, its chapel and lodgings that had for so long had a Benedictine presence, would no longer have that presence. It signaled the eventual closure of the farming enterprise in the future, a scenario that quite a few other monasteries throughout the country underwent in the second half of the twentieth century. Father Dominic, as farm boss, was able to provide assistance to the communities in Idaho and Cuernavaca with respect to the use of their land. For the monks, however, the long tradition of maintaining a self-sufficient agricultural complex was effectively ended.

6. Chapter minutes of October 28, 1975.
7. See *Mount Angel Letter* (February 1976), 5.

Abbot Anselm insisted on maintaining monastic observance. As an aid to this, he restructured the formation program, requiring five years of monastic formation for those in temporary vows. Father Bonaventure Zerr was made novice master and director of candidates in 1974. He was replaced in 1977 by Fr. Peter Eberle, who had returned from studies in Rome. Father Edmund Smith was appointed as prior. A liturgy committee, with Fr. Thomas as chair, was formed in 1977, divided into theological, pastoral, and ritual subcommittees. Abbot Anselm also spearheaded the first effort to produce a written customary of the monastery's practices, a product of his last year as abbot.

One of the discouraging aspects of Abbot Anselm's six years as abbot was the departure from the community of a number of monks. The fact that a similar exodus was taking place in other monasteries and religious communities did not lessen the impact this had on morale and the spirit of the house.

In actuality, the numbers in the monastic community remained strong. In 1968, there were over 110 monks (including those not in solemn vows) associated with Mount Angel. In 1980 that number was still over one hundred, and counting the members in Idaho and Mexico, there were still 120 monks. But the number of those entering was on the decline and the median age of the monastery was on the rise. In addition, there were twenty-one Mount Angel monks (not belonging to the dependent priories) who were living permanently outside of the monastery in 1980.

Another burden Abbot Anselm had to bear was a public case of embezzlement on the part of the abbey's first lay business manager, Dominic Faessler. An audit in 1977 discovered irregularities in accounts. Faessler was indicted in 1976 on two counts of bribery and convicted on one count of bribery in early 1978.[8] Once again, the accounts in the local press did not portray Mount Angel in a light of fiscal responsibility. A benefit of this incident, however, was the establishment of the abbey's first development office in March of 1979.

Not all the publicity attached to Mount Angel was negative. In 1975 the Nobel Prize-winning author, Alexander Solzhenitsyn, visited Mount Angel, in conjunction with the Old Believers Russian Community that

8. *Capital Journal*, Salem (January 19, 1978), 1.

Abbot Anselm and Fr. Bonaventure Zerr on either side of Russian
writer Alexander Solzhenitsyn during visit to Mount Angel, 1975.

had a spiritual connection with the Tikhvin Center and with Mount
Angel's Br. Ambrose.[9] Father Bonaventure Zerr, ever the linguist and
man of eclectic interest, recounted how he spoke with Solzhenitsyn
over several hours during his visit to Mount Angel on June 14.

The period of the 1970s was one when Mount Angel engendered a
new attraction for artists and environmentalists. Father Frederic De
Buyst, a monk of St. Andrew's Abbey in Belgium and a noted church
architect and editor of *Art d'Eglise,* was invited to teach in the seminary summer school in 1976. He advised the monastic community on
the renovation of the abbey church. This was the period when "the
Fort," an art studio situated next to the Aalto Library, became a place
for monks such as Br. Nathan Zodrow and Br. Claude Lane to begin to
do work on ceramics and iconography. A number of monks exhibited
interest in calligraphy, and the abbey and library started workshops
in this traditionally monastic skill. Still going strong at this time was
the Benedictine Art Shop that Fr. Hildebrand Melchior began and expanded at St. Mary's Parish in Mt. Angel during the course of his time
as pastor. In May of 1973 an environmental conference was hosted by

9. Brother Ambrose Moorman was the community member in charge of the
Tikhvin Center in the 1970s and the link with the Old Believers Russian Community in Oregon.

A photo taken immediately after the abbatial election of June 6, 1980: from left to right, Abbot Raphael DeSalvo, president of the Swiss-American Congregation, Abbot Bonaventure Zerr, and Abbot Anselm Galvin.

Mount Angel, where internationally-known scholar René Dubos spoke. Given the ecological awareness that was a hallmark of the Northwest in these years, it is not surprising that the monastic community became more attuned to it.

There was a regular visitation of the community in April of 1980. As had been the case in previous years, the visitators identified divisions within the community and a collective unease with the condition of both of the priories in Mexico and Idaho. Ultimately, Abbot Anselm came to the conclusion that a new person would be more adept as the community's abbot. Once Abbot Anselm had announced his resignation, the decision was made to have the community undergo a communal discernment led by Br. Ronald Fogarty, prior to the community's election of a new abbot. This discernment process was one more example of a more collaborative investment in determining the type of leadership the community wanted to have as a standard in the present and the future.

A Different Profile of Prayer and Work

The monastic community sensed that the abbatial election that took place on June 6, 1980, would be a pivotal one. The person chosen by the chapter was Fr. Bonaventure Zerr. He had grown up in Portland during World War II, his father having relocated there from South Dakota. He was a member of Sacred Heart Parish, one of the Portland parishes in the care of Mount Angel monks. He spent three years in the high school and college seminary at Mount Angel before entering the novitiate of the abbey in 1956. The lone sibling of Fr. Bonaventure became a member of the Queen of Angels Monastery, Sr. Jerome. After his ordination to the priesthood in 1962, Fr. Bonaventure followed in the footsteps of many other Mount Angel monks and was sent to Europe for further studies. In this case it was to the University of Munich. From 1962 to 1969 he completed advanced theological and biblical studies there. He resided at the Abbey of Saint Boniface, and by the time he finished his studies in 1969 he was proficient in German and had achieved status as a biblical scholar. The monks of Saint Boniface had suffered from the partial destruction of their monastery and church during World War II and gratefully accepted the help that was given them through the relief work of Fr. Alcuin. So they had special occasion to provide hospitality for the Scripture student from Mount Angel Abbey, and there continued to be a close bond between the two houses even before the election of Abbot Bonaventure.

Since his return to Mount Angel in 1969, Abbot Bonaventure gave indication of his incredible range of interests and intensity of energy. He served the community as subprior, novice master, assistant dean in the seminary, acquisitions librarian, and above all as a teacher in Sacred Scripture and theology. To attempt an adequate description of Fr. Bonaventure's intellectual range is no easy feat. His encyclopedic knowledge of the American Civil War, his wide-ranging reading interests, and his openness to new frontiers of study impressed those both inside and outside the monastery. Perhaps his signal contribution to the community before his election was his translation of the psalms for Paulist Press, which became the version utilized by the Mount Angel community in their Divine Office.[10] Given how many communities

10. Bonaventure Zerr, *The Psalms: A New Translation* (New York: Paulist Press, 1979). From August 29, 1973, all of the psalms in the Divine Office at Mount Angel were the ones of Abbot Bonaventure's translation. In 1987 Abbot Bonaventure, with the help of Fr. Augustine, did most of the work in the restructured scheme of the psalter used for the Divine Office.

Abbot Bonaventure Zerr with his mother and sister after his
blessing, August 28, 1980.

went through continual changes in their Liturgy of the Hours in the
last two decades of the twentieth century, it is remarkable that Abbot
Bonaventure's translation and the music accompanying it have served
the community well up to the present day.

Once in office, Abbot Bonaventure did his best to implement recommendations of the 1980 visitation and to visit the dependent communities in Idaho and Mexico. In Idaho he began the process of having
the monks concentrate their mission to one of hospitality. There was
a push on the part of the monks of Ascension to build a retreat facility, which they realized in 1994. They wanted as well to establish their
independence from Mount Angel. This they did in a canonical way on
August 3, 1998, when they became an independent conventual priory.

The monks in Cuernavaca were under the leadership of Fr. Louis
Chavet for most of the period of the 1980s. They were able to make
great progress on their new church and made inroads into hospitality
services and expanded their agricultural projects. Avocado trees now
became a principal crop and source of income for the community.

Abbot Bonaventure restored the practice of sending monks to Europe for study,[11] and in another return to a previous custom reduced the

11. Abbot Jeremy Driscoll and Prior Konrad Schaefer were the first to be sent
again to Europe under Abbot Bonaventure, a decision he made within the first
month of his being abbot.

formation period between simple profession and solemn profession to three years. He also made a series of new administrative appointments in the monastery, bringing in new faces as prior and novice master (Fr. Peter Eberle), business manager (Fr. Andrew Baumgartner) and junior master/choirmaster (Fr. Paschal Cheline).

Abbot Bonaventure bolstered the oblates of the abbey by appointing Fr. Bernard Sander as the oblate director in January of 1981. With Fr. Bernard's deep-set connections to so many layers of the wider Mount Angel family, the number of oblates and the degree of their involvement reached unprecedented levels in the decade of the 1980s. This was paralleled by the launch of an oblate program at Ascension monastery in Idaho that would blossom in future years.

A liturgical and logistical question that had created division in the community for some time was that of what to do with the main altar and baldachino in the abbey church in light of the changes that had been made after the Second Vatican Council. Some in the community wanted to remove the main altar and tabernacle, while others thought it was an essential component to the devotional and monastic tradition of the house. In the course of the deliberation, Abbot Bonaventure made the decision to do away with both the main altar and baldachino in 1981–82 and remove the Blessed Sacrament to a side altar.

In addition to the church renovations, Abbot Bonaventure saw to the much-needed renovation of Anselm Hall and the overhaul of the interior of the gymnasium that had suffered major damage from a fire. Another conference level was added to the retreat house as well, the last major renovation there before the major addition of 2018–19.

A measure of the change that took place with Abbot Bonaventure's abbatial tenure was the decision to cut back on the parish commitments the community had acquired over the years. The parish church in nearby Tillamook, one the abbey had served since 1917, was given over to the Archdiocese of Portland. So, too, a pair of parishes on the Pacific coast, St. Joseph Church in Cloverdale and St. Mary's by the Sea in Rockaway, were turned over to the Archdiocese of Portland. The counsel that Archbishop Gross had given almost a century before about being reluctant to take on parish commitments was being heeded.

One formidable task awaiting Abbot Bonaventure was that of celebrating the centennial of the monastery's founding. A series of events in 1981–82 were held to commemorate this. Abbot Bonaventure gave the

New altar in church blessed by Abbot Bonaventure, February 21, 1982.

community retreat in 1981. Mount Angel hosted the General Chapter of the Swiss-American Congregation from August 8–12 of that year. The solemn celebration of the centennial took place October 29–31, 1981. On that occasion Abbot Leonard Boesch of Engelberg Abbey was present. As a gesture of solidarity with the Mount Angel community, Abbot Leonard formally remitted the $75,000 debt that was still owed to the Swiss motherhouse, reiterating the ties of affection between the two monastic houses and asserting that "the two monasteries . . . will remain in the future united to one another in friendship and will stand by one another in time of need as best they can."[12] In 1982 Abbot Jerome Hanus, the abbot president of the Swiss-American Congregation and a monk of Conception Abbey, preached at a eucharistic celebration that ended the centennial year. In his homily he lauded Abbot Anselm Villiger for his willingness to support both Conception and Mount Angel in their road to independence, despite the many setbacks and

12. Document on "The Condition of the Debt of Mount Angel to the Abbey of Engelberg, Switzerland, as of 1 October, 1981," November 6, 1981. From an abbatial posting of Abbot Bonaventure in Mount Angel Abbey Archives (hereafter MAAA).

difficulties that were part of their story.[13] Looking back at the century since the founding, one can demonstrate how the relationship between Mount Angel and Engelberg was preserved by the gracious hospitality that the Swiss community afforded all Mount Angel monks who visited them. Whatever strains between the two communities that had once existed in previous years, by the centennial observance they were decidedly a thing of the past.

Joining the monks in the celebration of the centennial were the Benedictine women of the Queen of Angels Monastery. Although there were fewer examples of shared apostolic activity between the two communities than had been the case in the early history, the centennial rightly celebrated the role that the Benedictine sisters had played in the material and spiritual growth of Mount Angel Abbey. The monks, of course, continued to serve as chaplains for the Queen of Angels community, and they gave human and material support to their Mission Benedict, Casa Adele and St. Joseph Shelter, serving social justice needs in the town of Mt. Angel.

The library at this time initiated a series of lectures and special exhibits that highlighted its role as a cultural and intellectual showpiece for the region. Abbot Bonaventure encouraged the acquisition of rare books and the library's permanent collection grew accordingly. Abbot Bonaventure was a known bibliophile. On returning from trips to Europe he would bring back volumes of books that found their way to the library and many other outlets. Elements of the new and the old from the monastery assisted Abbot Bonaventure in this effort. Father Martin brought his expertise from over a half-century of working with the collection, and Fr. Hugh Feiss supplied a keen eye and energy for widening the range and fortifying the quality of holdings. An Abbey Art Commission was established as one more expression of the community's desire to enhance its aesthetic identity. Father Nathan Zodrow was named as curator of art for the abbey.

Another area of intense activity in the 1980s was the work of stabilizing the administrative structure and the enrollment of the seminary. Father Thomas O'Donnell replaced Fr. James Ribble as the rector of the School of Theology in 1982. Father Terrence Fitzgerald succeeded

13. Homily of Abbot Jerome, MAAA.

O'Donnell in 1984. Father Fitzgerald was a seminary alumnus and that seemed to help in developing his leadership style. The monastery saw its seminary apostolate occupying an increasingly vital role for the church in the Northwest. New pastoral and spiritual programs of formation were put in place. The Hispanic Ministry Program continued to grow in scope. In 1980 qualified persons other than Roman Catholic seminarians were allowed acceptance into graduate programs in theology. Coterminous with this, the composition of the student body was becoming more diverse, representing some of the ethnic variegation of the Pacific Rim.

Change was taking place in the leadership of the archdiocese coincident with the monastery. In 1986 Archbishop Cornelius Power's retirement was accepted, and Archbishop William Levada was named as his replacement. Archbishop Levada, as a "California outsider," found Abbot Bonaventure to be just the person he needed to be informed of the workings of the archdiocese and the role of Mount Angel in the ecclesial life of the Catholic Church in the Portland area. The new archbishop followed in the footsteps of his predecessors with frequency of visits to the hilltop and formed a strong friendship with Abbot Bonaventure. Archbishop Levada affirmed his allegiance to the work of the monastery by sending his seminarians to Mount Angel and encouraging bishops of surrounding dioceses to do the same. The Archbishop taught a course in ecclesiology at the seminary to reinforce his support.[14]

Another Shadow of Scandal

Just as Mount Angel was immersed in the course of church renewal and cultural conflict in the decades of the 1960s through the 1980s, so it came to know the fallout of the clerical sexual abuse scandal in the Catholic Church. During these decades several Mount Angel monks engaged in instances of sexual abuse of minors and others that came to light in subsequent years. Adequate structures for protection of youth and oversight of community members were lacking in these years, as they were in other religious communities and church institutions. The mindset of those who held administrative responsibility for monks

14. Telephone interview with Cardinal William Levada, August 3, 2019.

between 1960 and 1990 was one that lacked the skill set of pastoral sensitivity to victims and their families and the assertiveness needed to remove from ministry those who were accused of the abuse.

The perpetrators of sexual abuse were monks who were involved in the entire fabric of community work—parish life, the schools, and even new foundations. The impact this had internally on the monastic community is hard to measure. Once the nature of the sexual abuse was made known, the monastic community had to deal with a barrage of media coverage that tarnished the moral character of the community considerably. The daily public buffeting from the public press was a cross all had to bear. This was compounded by the reality of the financial crisis created by the payouts the community knew would be forthcoming in justice to the victims and their families.

One of the results of the public nature of this misconduct and the moral failure it registered was a commitment of the community to provide pastoral care to those who were the victims of such abuse and to implement programs in the seminary and throughout the ministerial network of Mount Angel's apostolates that would insure the highest levels of adherence to church law and new protocols of protection established by outside agencies.

Though the full weight of the scandal and the adverse publicity engendered by it did not have its effect until the first decade of the twenty-first century, one can assert that it left reverberations in the community akin to those of the fires of 1892 and 1926. Unlike those two previous tragedies, there was a moral blame to be affixed inside the community with the sexual abuse scandal, marked by sins of commission and omission. At the same time, like the previous devastation of the fires, the scandal set the monastery and the seminary on a new path, one committed to a change of structures and formation so as to never have the scandal replicate itself.

The Death of an Abbot

Abbot Bonaventure was not in good health for the last years of his abbatial tenure. Many confreres and friends noted how tired he seemed, but they attributed that to a grueling work schedule and heavy load of travel. He was diagnosed with cancer in early June of 1988 and died on June 22. The suddenness of Abbot Bonaventure's death took many by surprise. It was also a wholesome reality check of how laden with duty and stress the office of abbot had become.

Abbot Bonaventure, much like Abbot Damian, was in high demand on the "retreat circuit" for religious and monastic communities. In like manner, he was pressed into service to give talks and provide his expertise in the wider monastic world. At a community visitation in 1983 concern had been registered about the health of the abbot, even suggesting that he undergo a physical exam.[15] At the same visitation, there was a repeat of an often-heard theme in Mount Angel history of overwork. It may be that the abbot would be the figure who left his monks with the most graphic reminder of the potentially grave consequences of overwork.

Any summary of Abbot Bonaventure's contribution to the community must affirm the place he made for a vibrant intellectual life. Not everyone would see a comfortable fit with a Scripture scholar and superior, but Abbot Bonaventure made a compelling case for it. The fact that he sent Fr. Konrad Schaefer to the Pontifical Biblical Institute in Rome and to the École Biblique in Jerusalem to earn a doctorate, and that Fr. Konrad later became superior at the Cuernavaca community while teaching Scripture in the major seminary in Mexico City, attests to the workableness of that combination. Whether it was Toronto or Rome, Abbot Bonaventure was convinced of the value of having Mount Angel monks imbibe the complex cultures of intellectual life on a global scale and then give back in kind as teachers and authors.

The cultural and spiritual walls of Mount Angel were broadened as a result of Abbot Bonaventure's presence as monk and abbot. His legacy was to inject an authentic spiritual and fatherly voice, by turns to affirm the overall mission of Mount Angel and to challenge monks in their advance of the mission. His manner of staying engaged with the wide network of Mount Angel benefactors and friends, while at the same time maintaining his contacts with colleagues in academia and in the global monastic community, was a unique and lasting legacy for the monks and lay faithful alike.

15. Visitation report of 1983, Swiss-American Congregational Archives (SACA).

Transition and Transformation

Much as Prior Anselm had provided a reliable and supportive presence for Abbot Damian during his last years as abbot, Fr. Peter Eberle performed a similar function for Abbot Bonaventure in his last years. Thus, it was not surprising that the Mount Angel community elected Fr. Peter as abbot on August 10, 1988. The nephew of Fr. Luke, he had monastery postings similar to many of his predecessors. He had obtained an advanced degree in moral theology in Rome. On his return from studies in 1977, he was entrusted with the challenging task of novice master, as well as instructor in the seminary. With the election of Abbot Bonaventure in 1980, Fr. Peter was named as prior, while still retaining his role as novice master. The community he had entered as a novice had changed greatly.

The fortunes of Mount Angel in the last decade of the century were comparable to other houses of the Swiss-American foundation. In 1987 the number of monks in the community (including the priories in Mexico and Idaho) numbered over one hundred.

Abbot Peter Eberle at his blessing by Archbishop William Levada, September 10, 1988.

Abbot Jeremy with the community in Cuernavaca.

By the end of the century in 1999 that number was reduced to under ninety monks, even as the median age in Mount Angel and its satellite communities was rising.

This was a time of retrenchment in many monastic houses. Parishes were given up, and foundations made outside of the community closed. Among Swiss-American houses of monks, six new foundations in Latin America had been made in the course of the 1960s and 1970s. Monasteries in Peru (from St. Meinrad Archabbey) and in Belize (from Subiaco Abbey) were forced to close before the end of the century, and other houses saw reduced numbers of monks. The Cuernevaca community in the 1980s faced some of the challenges of these monasteries: a financial precariousness, a lack of human resources for formation, and a self-questioning about what particular type of work the priory should take on.

The staying power of the Cuernavaca community was reinforced by several circumstances in the 1990s. On August 2, 1991 the new monastery church was dedicated. It had been brought to completion through the efforts of a fellow Benedictine monk and noted architect, Fr. Gabriel Chavez de la Mora.[16] Father Konrad Schaefer was appointed to take over the reins of superior in 1995. The buildings and grounds of the priory continued to be enhanced. The former

16. See private compendium prepared by Prior Konrad Schaefer, August 3, 2019.

seminary dormitory was converted into a retreat house and soon began to attract people coming for spiritual direction, confession, and retreats. As more native vocations entered the monastery, they received advanced degrees. Monks began to teach at the local seminary of San José in Cuernavaca and the Pontifical University in Mexico City, and they took on increasing responsibilities in the retreat ministry.[17] The community achieved independent status as a conventual priory in 2017 and counted over twenty-five monks. This happened in the first year of Fr. Jeremy Driscoll becoming abbot of Mount Angel. When the Cuernavaca chapter elected Fr. Konrad as conventual prior, Abbot Jeremy presided at the election. The two monks who had been sent together to Rome for studies thirty-seven years earlier by Abbot Bonaventure could now recognize their mutual roles as religious head of their respective communities.

The status of Ascension Priory in Idaho underwent its own transformation in the last years of the second millennium. As mentioned previously, the land in Jerome needed to be prepared. Fathers Stephen Hoffman and Dominic Broxmeyer labored assiduously from 1977 to 1980 in constructing the new building for the monks. On October 14, 1992, the priory in Jerome broke ground for its new Ministry Center. By May of 1994, with construction completed, Abbot Peter presided at the blessing of the new center. He was joined by two of the people who had been present at the Mass held at the desert altar on the site thirty years earlier, retired Bishop Treinen and Bishop Emeritus Nicholas Walsh, along with Todd Brown, Bishop of Boise.[18]

It was clear at this stage that the priory's main service would be for retreats and programs of adult education and spirituality. In 1995 the priory filled the role of a service site for Elderhostel (now known as Road Scholar) programs. These programs continued as fixtures of the community and made the monastery known to a much larger base of people outside of Idaho. They bore witness to the ongoing discernment that took place among the monks.

The most significant step of the decade, however, was the decision of the members of the priory to become independent of Mount Angel,

---

17. Private compendium prepared by Prior Konrad Schaefer, August 3, 2019.

18. John O'Hagan, *Monastery of the Ascension, 1965–2015* (private printing, 2016), 81.

Photo of entrance to the Monastery of Nuestra Señora de los Angeles in Cuernavaca, Mexico.

made in 1998. That became official on August 3, 1998. Contemporaneous with this was the first election of a superior, Fr. Boniface Lautz. The community became known officially in that same year as the Monastery of the Ascension.

There were several other facets of the monastery that deserve mention. One was the oblate program. In March of 1983 the oblate program had begun under the guise of Fr. Simeon, with Fr. Joel Kehoe as director. By the end of the decade there were close to one hundred oblates, many involved in outreach programs to people in Idaho and as far away as Latin America. They were an active and prominent part of the Ascension Monastery witness.

There remained after independence a reciprocal sharing of monastic personnel with the mother abbey. Even though new membership came into the community, the monastery relied upon a monastic pipeline from Mount Angel for its leadership and spiritual ballast. An interesting turn of fortune took place when Fr. Joseph Wood, a member of the priory in 1997, was elected as abbot of Mount Angel in that same year.

Just as Mount Angel had gone to great lengths to promote the arts, so too did the Monastery of the Ascension. The most prominent example of this is found on the wall outside of the chapel. It is a mosaic of the ascension executed by Fr. Dennis Marx of Mount Angel. It is complemented inside the chapel by a foundation cross also crafted

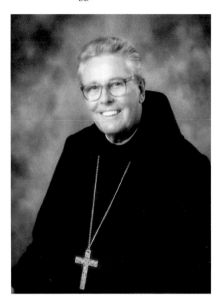

Abbot Joseph Wood (abbot from 1997 to 2001).

by Fr. Dennis. There are also two sets of Stations of the Cross, one of them located outdoors near the cemetery. These latter are bronze plaques designed by Ade Bethune, the renowned Catholic artist whose work adorns many Catholic churches and publications. The other set of stations in the monastery chapel was designed and executed by Br. Sylvester Sonnen of the priory.[19]

Also deserving of mention is the library assembled at the monastery. Father Augustine DeNoble of Mount Angel graciously donated time and expertise to establish the first library at Twin Falls. In succeeding years, the library's holdings were augmented by the donations of books from diocesan priests and from the Mount Angel Library. After the move to Jerome, an anonymous donor gave over $300,000 for the expansion of the library facility.[20] Another boon to the monastery and its library was to have Fr. Hugh arrive in 1996 as a member of the community. As head of the library at Mount Angel for the previous decade and as a recognized monastic scholar, he broadened the library holdings even more. It holds the distinction of having the largest collection of theological literature in the state of Idaho and, through its digital catalog, has widened its accessibility.

The monks of Idaho would not grow in number more than the dozen or so they counted when they became independent. They were blessed with the leadership of Fr. Boniface as prior for over twenty years and then Fr. Kenneth Hein. Their steady presence of hospitality and their efforts to mobilize the local population on issues as various as

19. O'Hagan, *Monastery of the Ascension*, 119–21.
20. O'Hagan, *Monastery of the Ascension*, 127.

ecological preservation and adult education initiatives won the admiration of a large ecumenical body of people grateful for their presence in southern Idaho.

Mount Angel served as a "feeder" to its two dependent foundations for some time, even as it began to cope with the reality of reduced numbers in the ranks of the motherhouse. But even as the numbers of monks at Mount Angel were diminishing, their range of ethnicity and background were giving the monastery a very different look. By the 1990s, for the first time, Vietnamese and Asian-American, Mexican, and Filipino members gave a greater diversity to the makeup of the community. Looking at the composition of the abbey after more than a century of its existence, one could notice how the monks had come full circle from the provincial and ethnically-closed community that had come to Oregon in 1882. In this case the hilltop monastery became an accurate image of the changing demographics in the Catholic Church in the Northwest and in the entire North American continent.

CHAPTER SEVEN

Ongoing Monastic Witness

A S MOUNT ANGEL ABBEY made its transition from one century and millennium to another, the evolution of several different areas of the community's mission were at play, ones that manifested the legendary Benedictine trait of adaptation to new ways, drawing from the storehouse of their long history. By undertaking a review of some of the abbey's main areas of influence and through studying segments of its history that reflect how they adapted to the circumstances of the time, a better understanding of the overall witness of the community may be gained.

The Seminary Apostolate

The original impetus for the community's presence in Oregon was closely tied to the immigrant population and their needs for education and sacramental assistance. This was at one with the larger Benedictine experience in North America up to that time. The educational component of that presence from the beginning included both a seminary education and a broader-based element of a secondary school that was open to students in trades and business, as well as in liberal arts. Over the course of the second half of the twentieth century the nature of that educational presence underwent some shifts. The closure of the college after World War II was in retrospect a prudent decision, one that allowed for a greater concentration of resources on the seminary. The same can be said for the closing of the prep school and the high school seminary in the decade after the Second Vatican Council. The community read the signs of the times accurately and prudently. As volatile and unpredictable as seminary programs were in the period after the council, Mount Angel found a way to maneuver through the new challenges that were presented. Its changing of the composition of its oversight board, its willingness to entrust the key position of rector to people outside the monastic community, its commitment to strengthen the evaluation mechanisms for seminarians, its outreach to a more diverse student body in age and ethnic background, and its commitment to a thorough pastoral formation all helped advance the seminary's status in the estimation of a wider public.

The fact that there was a continuous monastic presence on the faculty and in the spiritual formation of the seminarians was one more reason for the seminary to ride out many of the waves of change that roiled other diocesan seminaries. That presence included women from the Benedictine community of Queen of the Angels. The mutual respect exchanged between the archbishops of Portland and the abbots of Mount Angel stands as yet another reason for the maintenance of a high caliber of seminary education over time.

Historically speaking, the monastery's commitment to seminary work aligned well with its membership in the Swiss-American Congregation of monks. Three of the four largest monasteries in the congregation stayed the course of conducting an apostolate of seminary education. It bears mention that the vigor of Mount Angel's foundation in British Columbia of Westminster Abbey and its seminary program can be traced to the model of seminary ministry they received from the motherhouse. The identity of Mount Angel with its work of theological and spiritual formation remains in the forefront of its historical narrative.

Hospitality

Another example of creative adaptation of a community work is that of hospitality. Once the community had moved to the hilltop in 1903, there was a perception on the part of laity, seminarians, and priests that this was a holy space where people of faith could come and find spiritual nourishment. It is to Abbot Damian's credit that he detected this need early on and in his time as abbot made it possible to formalize

Seminary Rector Fr. Patrick Brennan with students.

Fr. Gregory Duerr with seminary students, 1981.

Abbot Jeremy Driscoll welcoming visitors to St. Benedict Festival in July 2016.

a commitment to hospitality with the construction of a guesthouse. Few would dispute the fact that from 1960 on, the continuous use of the guesthouse by priests, pilgrims, oblates, and guests has made Mount Angel a genuine spiritual center for the region. The subsequent improvements and additions to the guesthouse, culminating with the rededication of the expanded facility in June of 2019, gave proof of how the Mount Angel community stayed on the cutting edge of serving the needs of the wider community. It also indicated how the community had discerned that a conscious and consensual commitment to serve the needs of guests was in the forefront of Mount Angel's monastic witness.

An example of a new and innovative expression of such hospitality began in July of 2014 with the Saint Benedict Festival. It was an occasion when the entire open space of the hilltop was filled with monks and volunteers of the abbey offering the resources of the community to visitors and highlighting the interaction between monastic hosts and the guests. The resources for helping in this included books and beer, iconographic art and ethnic foods. Most pointedly, it included an invitation to join in the prayer life of the abbey community, to begin and end the day. It was a venue that took advantage of the beauty of

Visitors assembled in abbey church for St. Benedict Festival in 2016.

Fr. Philip Waibel at calligrapher booth for St. Benedict Festival, 2016.

the grounds and buildings and had as a central attraction the monks in the role of hosts. It now appears to be a fixture of a July Saturday when the hilltop space receives hundreds of visitors.

Despite the prohibition era and many temperance advocates that have surrounded it over the years, the town of Mt. Angel has been closely associated with its fall Octoberfest, featuring beer and German foods. In recent years, a similar old and revered monastic custom of beer production was adapted in the creation by the monks of Mount Angel of the Benedictine Brewery. Connections of Mount Angel's past came together in this enterprise. Assistance after World War II given to the Bavarian Abbey of Andechs, famous for its beer, helped to trigger the idea of importing a similar product in the United States. The long history of the cultivation and harvesting of hops associated with Mount Angel created an appropriate setting for the work of brewing, as did the wells on the property that supplied the water for the brewing process. Certainly, the German and continental tradition of the beer garden and the Benedictine history of making beer came together with the abbey's promotion of its own beer product and a place on the grounds, St. Michael's Taproom, for visitors to relax and share the product. Living in the midst of a region of the Northwest where craft beers held sway, Mount Angel clearly claimed a niche with a brand that people knew stood for New World quality and Old World taste. The fact that all of this transpired one hundred years after prohibition had prevented the abbey hops from finding their way into brewed beverages made the adaptation all the more pointed.

A concordant development in the area of hospitality, one that occurred throughout the monastic world in the period after 1980, was a precipitate rise in the number and participation of Benedictine oblates. Recognition of this phenomenon on the part of superiors and the appointment of such capable oblate directors as Fr. Bernard at Mount Angel and Fr. Hugh at Ascension serves as another testament to a sensitive discernment of the needs of the faithful. It allowed a much broader and committed group of laity to be integrated into the broad monastic mission of Mount Angel.

It came as no surprise that two of the three foundations of Mount Angel in the twentieth century, the Monastery of the Ascension in Idaho and Our Lady of the Angels Monastery in Cuernavaca, both took on this same work of hospitality as their principal ministry. They truly

Fr. Martin Grassel, Abbey
Brewmaster, inspecting hops.

became centers of spiritual renewal and formation as they attracted
diverse groups of people to their sacred space. In many aspects, the
role of the monastery in its formative years had been one of monks
going out to parishes and mission posts to spread the faith. Generations later, in a cyclical historical turn, the people were being drawn
to the monastery to find the spiritual fulfillment.

Models of Leadership

Another area where Mount Angel gave evidence of a consistent and
contributing role in the church and in the world was its leadership. Its
abbots, diverse in gifts and personality, seemed to provide a style and
service that fit well for their time. Early examples of that would include
Abbot Frowin's responsible and solicitous stewardship of the community in its difficult passage from 1898 to 1918, and Abbot Placidus and
Abbot Bernard's conscientious and creative tenures from 1910 to 1934.

During the period of greatest material growth and stabilization,
1934–74, Abbots Thomas Meier and Damian Jentges made bold decisions and exercised keen oversight when unprecedented demands were
being made on the community. These two men by turns were visionary
and materially responsible stewards from whom the monastic community drew wisdom and good sense.

Abbot Nathan Zodrow served as abbot of Mount Angel from 2001 to 2009.

When one looks at the alternation of abbatial successors of Abbot Damian, from Abbot Anselm and Abbot Peter through Abbot Joseph Wood and Abbot Nathan Zodrow, one is struck by the variety of leadership styles and the breadth of experience each of these men brought to their tenure. The charismatic and scholarly Abbot Bonaventure had on either side of him, in Abbots Anselm and Peter, men who were steeped in the wide range of Mount Angel apostolic work. Abbot Joseph represented well the many monks who had spent much of their time outside the community in parish life, whereas Abbot Joseph's two successors, Abbot Nathan and Abbot Gregory, were known for their involvement in the seminary and the monastery.

The leadership extended beyond the boundaries of Mount Angel's cloister. After his resignation, Abbot Peter was elected as president of the Swiss-American Congregation and served two terms in that role from 1999 to 2011. The same congregation benefited from the services of Fr. Paul Thomas as member of the Legal Committee and President's Council. Before he became abbot, Fr. Jeremy Driscoll served as an advisor to the *Vox Clara* committee that the Vatican charged with new English translations for liturgical texts. As of this writing he is also in his third five-year term as a papally-appointed advisor to the Vatican's Congregation on Liturgy.

Outside abbatial leadership, the outstanding example of an individual monk leaving a lasting imprint on the community and wider church was Fr. Alcuin Heibel. His personal initiative in launching a Benedictine community in Mexico and his singular mission of organizing and delivering relief to war-torn parts of Europe after World

War II remain noteworthy on several accounts. They reflect the willingness of Mount Angel to see and venture beyond its immediate geographic compass. At the same time, it serves as a compelling example of superiors being willing to place monks in the service of the wider church.

Father Alcuin proved to be a goodwill ambassador for the monks of Mount Angel in surprising ways. Abbot Bonaventure recounted how as a student in residence at Saint Boniface monastery in Munich, the monks of that community spoke fondly of the largesse and kindness they experienced from Fr. Alcuin when he visited them after World War II.

Abbot Gregory Duerr served as abbot of Mount Angel from 2009 to 2016.

Parishioners from Sacred Heart parish in Portland, State Department personnel, and Peace Corps volunteers all remembered what they described as the remarkable energy and people skills of Fr. Alcuin.

Extraordinary, too, was the long-term duration of monks in important leadership roles. Notice of Fr. Martin's uncommon stretch of over twenty-five years as prior was made earlier. That was of a piece with one of his predecessors as prior, Fr. Jerome, who served faithfully for over two decades. There seemed to be something of the same pattern at work in the houses founded by Mount Angel. At Westminster, Abbot Eugene served as superior (both as prior and abbot) for over forty years. At the Monastery of Ascension, Fr. Boniface served for over two decades in his first time as superior and was elected again in 2016. Father Konrad in Cuernevaca has served for almost twenty-five years as superior. Such long periods of governance reflect not only a remarkable sense of duty, but a satisfaction on the part of the community with the leadership they receive.

The Old and the New

In their first service to the needs of the populace surrounding them in the Willamette Valley, there was a pronounced preference for German-speaking Catholics. One can see, especially in the development of the Press, that there was an express obligation to educate and form opinion of the faithful. The *St. Josephs Blatt* and *Armen Seelen Freund* reflect this most clearly. When the German-language publications were dropped in the 1970s the time of their influence had long passed. But the influence of the Press remained significant for most of the twentieth century as a service to Catholics and a revenue producer for the community. With respect to its function as a resource for the community and the Benedictine world, the Press was invaluable for spurring the fundraising for the abbey after the disastrous fire of 1926. It remained for the first half of the twentieth century the principal means of communicating the message of Mount Angel's work to a wider public. That was accomplished not only through *St. Joseph Magazine* but also through publications that conveyed the monastic identity of the community, such as the catalogs of the schools through the years and the Swiss-American Congregation's documents such as *Declarations and Constitutions*.[1] Mount Angel was firmly in the tradition of its fellow Benedictine houses in this regard, particularly the Abbey Press at St. Meinrad and the Altar and Home Press at Conception. When the Press finally closed in 2002, it was a recognition that the digital age and the demands being made of the monastery required new modes of communication. Yet there was left a legacy of a respect for the written word that registered in everything from the calligraphy lessons taught by monks and laypersons to the impressive armoire of printed books in the Aalto Library and the practice still retained in the monastic refectory of having reading at meals twice a day.

Another symbol of the early days of Mount Angel that was of a piece with the people it served was the considerable agricultural complex that evolved. The abbey farm, with its dairy herd, beef cattle, and pigs, its large acreage of hops, grain and hay, and its vast holdings of trees was something of a model for surrounding farmers, akin to a

---

1. *Declarationes in Sacram Reglam et Constitutiones* (Mount Angel Abbey, 1950).

medieval monastery's manor. In this respect, Mount Angel carved out its own corporate example of stewardship. The methods of cutting and replanting of the abbey's tree holdings, the skill in discovering underground water sources for well-drilling sites, and the prudent use of irrigation can be posited as examples of responsible care for the land. It was an agricultural economy that depended upon a sizeable and pliant monastic work force and sound management. In the case of Mount Angel, their history has an abundance of examples of these upon which to draw: an image of Fr. Jerome Wespe in his seventies, avidly sawing wood; Br. Fidelis faithfully feeding the chickens by hand; and the hop harvest each fall when the junior monks would bale the dried hops. But perhaps the foremost embodiment of the superior management and hard work that imbued Mount Angel's agricultural economy was that of Fr. Dominic Broxmeyer. From 1948 until 1976, Fr. Dominic was charged with overseeing the abbey farm. He did that with a diligence that impressed both confreres and fellow farmers and business associates in the Willamette Valley. Even after the farmlands were outsourced, Fr. Dominic remained a wise consultant for others

Bookstore and coffee shop.

on the best use of the land and crop rotation. What may have been the last vestige of that agricultural heritage was the large vegetable garden at the foot of the hilltop, a piece of land that Fr. Dominic cultivated with care almost to the time of his death in 2001.

One more example of bringing the new from the old was the conversion of the Benedictine Press building after its closure into a bookstore and coffee shop. For anyone alert to the Portland region's penchant for coffeehouses and bookstores, having guests feel at home in a place where the books and the beverages connect makes eminent sense. That is even more so when it includes the enjoyment of an atmosphere of peace within a monastic setting.

Symbols and Landmarks

Traces of Mount Angel's history are contained in some of the arresting symbols that are associated with the landscape. The outdoor stations of the cross that lead one from the base of the hill to its crest, crafted in Germany in the nineteenth century and gifted to the monks in their earliest days, still evoke the devotional period of the first generation of monks and the faithful. The cemetery and the oldest edifice of Mount Angel, the original pilgrimage chapel atop the hill, serve as icons of the passage of history from the founding period to the present. The figures of the Guardian Angel and the Sacred Heart of Jesus that stand on the lawn just north and south of the church are statues that survived the fire of 1926 and engender memories of that era. The statue of St. Joseph now in the monastic refectory remains a symbol of the strong devotion to St. Joseph that is remembered daily in the community's recitation of the Litany of St. Joseph.

Artistic expression of more recent vintage certainly includes the Aalto Library. It is not only a signature symbol of innovative modern design, but a building that has blended into the brick and the topography of the surrounding hilltop. Another architectural landmark that fills out the façade of the church is the bell tower, constructed in 2007 under Abbot Nathan's supervision. Standing 117 feet in height, the tower contains the largest peal of bells on the West Coast. It conveys both vertical solidity and the ancient monastic custom of announcing the time for prayer and the passage of the day. Interior symbols within

Abbey cemetery and pilgrimage chapel in winter of 2015.

Br. Claude Lane writing an icon.

The abbey church bell tower from the Guesthouse.

St. Joseph Statue in the
abbey refectory: a symbol
of community devotion to
St. Joseph.

Icon of Br. Claude over the abbot's table in the monastic refectory.

Entry of Annunciation Hall with icon of the Annunciation, 2016.

View from dining room of renovated guesthouse, 2019.

the cloister include the magnificent iconography of Br. Claude Lane done in the monastic refectory and throughout the house. Another revealing landmark of the twenty-first century is the seminary's classroom and office building, called simply "Annunciation." In its entrance one can admire a large mosaic of the annunciation designed by Br. Claude that draws from ancient art forms. Throughout the building, one can also admire the state-of-the-art environmental and technological innovations that remind the visitor of how monks and technology have never been adversaries. In 2019 a renovated and expanded guesthouse, another example of authoritative architecture, was dedicated. The building of the Aalto Library in 1970 set the standard for excellence in architecture for all that followed.

Pastoral Outreach

For the first generations of Mount Angel's existence, the presence of monks was felt most visibly and consistently in its sacramental supply and pastoral assistance to local communities. The aforementioned ministry to Native Americans took monks out of the country. Later requests made for a presence in Alaska over several decades. The number of parishes staffed and serviced by Mount Angel monks rose throughout the first part of the twentieth century. To these were added chaplaincies to the Benedictine Sisters and to the Mt. Angel Retirement Center, as well as to hospitals. The spiritual imprint left by monks who served these stations was considerable. Knowing that for some years the Mount Angel priest-monks were entrusted with all of the parishes in Tillamook County gives some indication of the breadth of their influence. Within the city of Portland, Sacred Heart and Saint Agatha parishes were two examples of a long-lasting Benedictine presence that helped to lay the seed for vocations to the monastic life and deepen the spirituality of the local church.

The mark of pastoral care left by Mount Angel monks was not limited to sacramental supply. Father Victor Rassier, when he was choirmaster, would conduct weekly classes in Gregorian chant for Catholic schools in Portland. He did that so successfully that he was named archdiocesan director of chant and met with requests from numerous religious orders of women to conduct chant classes for their communities.[2] As a pastor of St. Mary by the Sea Parish in coastal Oregon, long after his choirmaster duties, he taught chant and public speaking and encouraged liturgical participation, anticipating many of the changes that would be associated with the Second Vatican Council.

Earlier mention was made of the monks who served as chaplains for the Armed Forces in both world wars. Father Leo Rimmele served as an Air Force chaplain in Vietnam and in Germany from 1966 to 1974, receiving a Bronze Star for his service in Vietnam. Father Karl Nielson became a chaplain in the Naval Reserve in the 1980s.

Father Kenneth Jacques, a monk of the abbey who worked in the Philippines for the Vietnamese Apostolate in the 1980s, encountered there two Vietnamese Catholic "boat people" who had escaped from Vietnam. He befriended them, provided for their transport to the United States, and saw them placed in the seminary at Mount Angel. These two men, Fr. Thomas Dien Dung and Fr. Vincent Liem Nguyen, became the first of a number of Vietnamese monks who entered Mount Angel Abbey in the 1980s.

2. Necrology for February 15, 1964.

Monastic community before the abbey church during retreat of 2018.

From the 1970s on, the extent of Benedictine presence in parishes waned. This was reflective of an overall trend in houses of monks throughout the country. The era of the missionary monk and pastoral care circuit rider was being supplanted by a concentration on having monks see the abbey as center of their life and the monastic community as the focus of their energy.

Local parishes served by the monks for the first hundred years of Mount Angel's existence represented the ethnic persona of the monks—Caucasian and coming from the northern parts of Europe. In the last four decades, the immediate area around Mount Angel and the large geographic expanse of the Northwest have witnessed an explosion of Spanish-speaking and Asian faithful. The communities served by Mount Angel have mirrored this, and the complexion of the monks of Mount Angel is now very much reflective of this new ethnic diversity.

The Life of the Mind

In its early years, serious scholarship and cultivation of the life of the mind were given little apparent outlet at Mount Angel when contrasted with the demands of manual labor, pastoral care, and multiple assign-ments. A distinct advantage of sending monks away for study was to expose them to arenas of scholarship and academic excellence that would train them in the same qualities. A practical advantage of having secondary schools and the seminary was the need to have people earn graduate degrees so as to have the requisite qualifications to teach and administer. There were some brilliant minds who were recognized as such in their time. Father Augustine Bachofen was only one example of a person whose contributions to canon law commentary became a landmark for other scholars. There were also Scripture scholars who carved out their own special world of achievement. Father Jerome created a vocabulary of New Testament Greek in his years of teaching Scripture. Father Bonaventure may be the best representative of a free-form love of learning. His acknowledged scholarship in biblical studies was matched by his broad range of interests in other areas of study. Fathers Matthias, Konrad, and Thomas Thien Dang all carried from their biblical studies in Rome and Jerusalem a culture of deep study of the word of God that permeated the life around them.

In more recent times, the abbey has been blessed with monks who have achieved a niche in monastic and theological scholarship. Father Hugh Feiss, over his period of time at Mount Angel and Ascension Monastery, has authored a striking number of books for both the wider public and a more exclusive audience of monastic scholars.[3] Abbot Jeremy Driscoll, after receiving his doctorate in theology, began teaching both in Rome at Sant'Anselmo and at the seminary in Mount Angel. Beginning in the 1990s, he produced a steady line of books on spirituality and theology.[4] Having such scholars as teachers in the seminary

---

3. Two of the more popular works of Fr. Hugh are *Essential Monastic Wisdom: Writings on the Contemplative Life* (San Francisco: Harper Collins, 1999) and *A Benedictine Reader: 530–1530* (Collegeville, MN: Cistercian Publications, 2019).

4. Among the publications of Abbot Jeremy are *Evagrius Ponticus, Ad Monachus: Translation and Commentary*, Ancient Christian Writers (New York: Newman Press, 2003); "Monastic Culture and the Catholic Intellectual Tradition," in A. J. Cernera and O. J. Morgan, eds., *Examining the Catholic Intellectual Tradition* (Fairfield, CT: Sacred Heart University Press, 2000), 55–73; *What Happens at Mass* (Chicago: Liturgy Training Publications, 2005); *A Monk's Alphabet: Random Thoughts of a Monk in Alphabetical Order* (Boston: New Seeds, 2006); and *Awesome Glory: Resurrection in Scripture, Liturgy, and Theology* (Collegeville, MN: Liturgical Press, 2019).

as they were writing their books gave the scholarship an even more practical base.

The life of the mind invites inclusion of the musical talent that has run through the Mount Angel history from its very beginning. Father Domininc Waedenschwyler wrote original compositions for both secular settings (employing the first college orchestra) and church music. Abbot Placidus was known for his compositions of sacred music and for his amazing versatility with musical instruments, from keyboard to clarinet and banjo. Father David Nicholson may have the achievement of the most published works on music.[5] He did his writing of musical compositions and of musicology as he was in charge of music for the abbey and the Gregorian choir for the seminary. Father Dennis Marx, with his studies at Juilliard and the Toronto Conservatory, lent the perspective of a professional musician in all respects during his time as choirmaster in the 1970s. Brother Owen Alstott provided the community with an array of liturgical compositions in English during the period of renewal after Vatican II. And Br. Marius Walter in the 1990s achieved an excellence in creative vocal and instrumental works.

Dealing with Setbacks and Scandals

Throughout the arc of Mount Angel's history there has been a recurring round of unexpected and threatening events that have imperiled its development. At the head of a list of these events are the fires of 1892 and 1926. Both of these events were accompanied by a grave financial crisis and a full agenda of questions relating to the continued existence of the Mount Angel monastic community. In the case of the 1892 fire, the community was able to make the prudent and prescient choice of building anew on the hilltop rather than at its base. Another positive element that surfaced soon after the fire was Engelberg Abbey's decision to support and strengthen the monastic character of the Oregon community through the appointment of Fr. Benedict Gottwald and

5. Dom David Nicholson, *The Style and Interpretation of Gregorian Chant* and *Liturgical Music in Benedictine Monasticism: A Post-Vatican II Survey,* both published by Mount Angel Abbey.

Abbot Frowin Conrad as leaders who found a way to nurture a community that could otherwise easily have fractured. The fundraising campaign of Fr. Adelhelm undertaken in the wake of the fire had the added benefit of making Mount Angel known in parts of the country that previously had not heard of the community or its monks. The 1926 fire, more devastating in the scope of its damage, had the consequence of the monastic chapter reaffirming its desire to continue its monastic mission and galvanized the community into a building program that transformed the view of the hilltop. In the aftermath of the fire there was a surprising cessation of some of the nativist prejudice that until then had been a palpable part of the monastery's relationship with the surrounding communities.

In the terms of natural disasters, the community was spared anything approaching the seriousness of the first two fires. The earthquake of 1993 that damaged part of the structure of the apse of the church actually led to a more complete renovation of the sanctuary area that had already been in the planning stage.

Perhaps the scandal that triggered the most adverse press and presented the biggest cross to the community in its early years was the departure of Abbot Thomas Meienhofer as abbot in 1910. Given the fact that Abbot Thomas was the first abbot of the abbey and someone well-known in the Portland area, the news of his resignation from his office and the clandestine trip with the woman who would become his wife might appear to have been scripted by a writer of anti-Catholic tracts. It left the community reeling. But here, too, it served to have the monks of Mount Angel look more searchingly and honestly at the qualities of leadership they needed to see them through a dark time and the stages of their history since. In this one can say they were successful, given the caliber of monastic leaders chosen after 1910.

A scandal that came over a half-century later was of a very different sort. Father Hildebrand Melchior's Mount Angel Towers Project for the elderly was awash with good intentions. It aimed to provide a caring and Catholic retirement community, long before abbeys such as Mount Angel began to do the same. In the case of Mount Angel Towers, however, the ethos of the era influenced the planning. It was designed and constructed at the same time as the Great Society programs of President Johnson and shared in the grandiosity of its dimensions. In retrospect, one can say that it was too large a building for the needs of that time and the management and oversight functions of those who controlled the construction and direction of the project were sorely lacking. The entire project exuded the idealism and oversized expectations that so typified the 1960s. Looking back, criticism can be leveled at Fr. Hildebrand for his single-handed and hard-driven support of the project without bringing in some more seasoned hands and more extensive counsel.

Abbot Damian and members of the inner circle of the community should also have exerted more oversight on the project and on Fr. Hildebrand's involvement. But it did serve the purpose of later abbots when they were presented with scandals of people in the business office. Abbot Anselm had to face an instance of a lay business manager manipulating funds in the 1970s and revelations in 1997–98 determined that unauthorized loans had been pushed through the business office. There was some adverse publicity, but superiors responded with decisiveness in correcting the malfeasance.

What was arguably the most difficult challenge to the abbey and seminary, one it shared with the wider church, was the clerical sexual abuse scandal that fully emerged in the first decade of the twenty-first century. Even though the majority of the allegations of sexual abuse involving monks of Mount Angel took place in the second half of the twentieth century, the publicity attached to the accusations was concentrated in the year 2002 and following. Not unlike the fires of Mount Angel in the early years, the sexual abuse scandal created a financial crisis that undercut years of careful planning of budgets and fiscal responsibility. Even with insurance coverage, the restitution given to victims and their families went beyond any initial calculation. The more serious damage in question with this scandal, however, was the human toll. That was in the first place with regard to the victims of the abuse and their families, whose immediate need for compassionate engagement was not always met. It also took its toll on the monks as a whole, the overwhelming majority of whom had no direct involvement with the abuse, but who bore the brunt of its consequences. There was a disproportionate burden placed on leadership, in this case on Abbot Nathan, who attempted to exhibit both justice and pastoral care for all concerned, while having to shoulder the legal implications for the monastery and the seminary. The coverage of the scandal in the secular press played itself out over a period of months and undermined for many the integrity and trust the abbey had enjoyed for many years. The scandal for the monastery was one that was shared with the archdiocese and other religious orders.[6] The abbey's situation was aggravated even more when the Archdiocese of Portland was included in lawsuits brought against the abbey.[7] Its negative effect was hard to fix in practical terms, but the immediate impact upon seminary enrollment, vocations to the monastery, and the morale of the community was clearly detrimental. The moral scar on the institution did not soon go away.

However, in this instance, as with the other previous challenges, there was evidence of grace occurring in the scandal's wake. As was the case with the Catholic Church in general after 2002, safeguards were set in place to ensure that protection of all people who were part of Mount Angel's pastoral responsibility would be a pledge that was kept. Stricter standards of training and spiritual/sexual formation became part of the protocol of abbey and seminary. The monks realized their common obligation to exhibit a more transparent witness of chaste life and to be vigilant in safeguarding their work of teaching and ministry. To assess how thoroughly this new initiative for protecting all people served by the abbey was integrated into the corporate life and ministry of the hilltop, one can refer to a three-part series published by the *National Catholic Reporter* in early 2019, holding up the Mount Angel Seminary's program of formation in celibate chastity as a model for others.[8]

The erosion of trust and the weakening of Mount Angel's spiritual witness occasioned by the clerical sexual abuse scandal in the first

6. The Society of Jesus in Oregon and Washington was especially hard hit with the scandal.

7. The community was fortunate to have the unambiguous support of the Portland archbishop at the time, John Vlazny. See the correspondence of Archbishop Vlazny with Abbot Nathan Zodrow, Mount Angel Abbey Archives (MAAA).

8. Dan Morris-Young, "Catholic Abuse Scandal Galvanizes Mount Angel Seminarians' Resolve," *National Catholic Reporter* (January 28, 2019); "Screening, Service, Reflection Are Mount Angel's Antidotes to Clericalism," *National Catholic Reporter* (February 8, 2019); and "Diversity at Mount Angel Enriches Formation," *National Catholic Reporter* (February 14, 2019).

decade of the twenty-first century presented a different type of crisis. A compelling argument can be made that the changes made in both the abbey and seminary in ensuing years were proactive and prudent means of confronting the crisis. The abbey relied upon committed and professional lay persons who offered advice and implemented programs that dealt with the underlying conditions that gave rise to the crisis. More scrutiny of candidates for the monastery and seminary and more exacting standards of spiritual and psychological formation were put into effect. Although the monks of Mount Angel suffered with the entire Catholic Church, it recognized after the fact that a sustained examination of its spiritual protocols for entrance and ministerial evaluation would be needed well into its future.

A Final Assessment

The history of any community with a spiritual or religious mission must be analyzed on two levels. These two levels may run parallel paths and intermittently intersect, but both are essential for a proper understanding of the ethos of the community's story and the human characters who are part of it.

The first level concerns the impact and influence of the monastery of Mount Angel as a social institution. A scrutiny of the social significance of Mount Angel must include the imprint it has left in its educational institutions. From the seminary's more than hundred years of uninterrupted formation on all of its levels to the college's healthy presence in the first part of the twentieth century, to the high school's presence in varying guises over eighty years, and to the Christie School for Native Americans, the personalized and professional effect of Mount Angel monks as both pedagogues and as mentors for many lay colleagues cannot be discounted. This classroom love of learning has been augmented in the course of time by an institutional commitment to cultivating the arts. There seems to have been no conscious plan of shaping such an institutional purpose, but the combination of deep European connections, a continuing corps of highly educated and skilled monks, and a growing abundance of material resources have forged a monastic culture of appreciation for the pursuit of truth and beauty.

A contemporary view from the air of the monastic complex of Mount Angel.

Another element of the institutional force of Mount Angel, one very much at the heart of its Benedictine legacy, has been its commitment to work and improve the land. Even though the external signs of the abbey's agricultural complex waned in the last half-century, the ideal of a self-sustaining monastic network of animal life, foodstuffs, and human stewardship of resources was brought to realization for the formative years of Mount Angel's history and remained a major component of its growth. In the face of so much change in the world around it from the years of its founding generation, the abbey still feels at home in the agricultural sprawl of the Willamette Valley and recognizes its role in modeling a care for the environment and its resources, one that upholds the best of Benedictine tradition.

In an era of globalized connectiveness, there should be no surprise over institutions that depend on global networks to ensure their social awareness and economic sustainability. In the case of Mount Angel, such global connectiveness was an ingrained institutional feature long before the advent of social media and the array of avenues of international communication. Mount Angel's position on the West Coast of the United States at the time of its founding could easily have lent itself to a community persona of institutional outlier. It was not to be. The strong solidarity with the home community of Engelberg and the many different European monasteries that came into the orbit of Mount Angel and its monks precluded any isolationism. Mount Angel definitely benefited from the universal character of Benedictine life on many continents. To see the presence of Mount Angel monks in Canada and Mexico already in the first half of the twentieth century indicates how this global sensibility was at work early in the community history. A level of comfort with the wide range of nationalities and geographically disparate groups that formed part of the monastery and seminary communities in recent years confirms the claim of a local institution for Oregon that developed an international face.

The second level upon which to assess Mount Angel's historical impact is harder to gauge, for it enters the realm of faith and spiritual witness. There is no doubt that the founding figures of Mount Angel, particularly Abbot Anselm Villiger of Engelberg and Fr. Adelhelm Odermatt, became iconic manifestations of a firm faith that the success of the new American monastery rested in the hands of God. Only when this faith is measured against the multiple challenges faced by the first generation of monks—large indebtedness, catastrophic fire, a divided membership within the community—can its weight be appreciated. Perhaps the outstanding example of how that faith was personified rests in the person of Abbot Frowin Conrad. To have seen the new community in Oregon begin its history as a publicly acknowledged antithesis of Abbot Frowin's own Abbey of Conception was a hard blow by any account. Yet it was Abbot Frowin, more than any other individual in the trying times of Mount Angel's early history, whose faith in the community and whose indefatigable efforts to transmit that faith in the monastic model he exhibited became the turning point in having Mount Angel acquire a requisite maturity and confidence to formulate an appropriate monastic identity.

Giving definition to a community's spiritual witness may be equally difficult to articulate. But it is rendered easier when it is connected to human figures who occupy the landscape of Mount Angel's history. Those figures have never been lacking. There is Fr. Adelhelm, gamely scouring parish and church communities throughout the country in search of money to keep Mount Angel afloat after the 1892 fire. There is Fr. Benedict Gottwald, stolidly accepting a most difficult obedience of leading a fractured community, undecided on where to rebuild, and imparting to it an example of monastic observance and of listening. There are the young priest-monks, Frs. Bernard Murphy and Jerome Wespe, investing deeply into a community beset by contention and becoming exemplars of monastic life and spiritual leaders as they helped form generations of monks and students. There is Br. Celestine Mueller, using the press as a vehicle for proclamation of the Gospel and for having people savor the monastic charism of Mount Angel. There is Br. Gabriel Loerch, painstakingly putting in place choir stalls that he must have known would outlast the lifetimes of all his confreres. There is Fr. Maurus Snyder, the last surviving member of the founding generation, making his rounds of the schools and shops in the 1950s, wanting to make sure that all was working well. There is Fr. Augustine DeNoble, determined to collect and preserve the historical record of the community even as he transmitted its oral version. The series of personal biographies given earlier in the text serve as another checklist for the variety of spiritual witnesses and the heroic if not saintly dimensions it could take on.

A goodly part of the spiritual witness defies codification. It was done collectively during the difficult times of financial austerity and performed individually with enough regularity to edify those inside and outside the cloister. It was a witness to the Benedictine vows taken by community members and a witness to Gospel values inherent in a Catholic institution like Mount Angel.

The knowledge that this spiritual witness flagged at times in the history of Mount Angel and was not as detectable in some monks as in others only affirms the importance of such a witness for the spiritual and psychological health of the total institution. The underlying current of determination to serve the Lord and the people of God through the framework of community was the constant in the story of Mount Angel. In the telling it allows the historian to see a sweep of observed good fruit derived from the community's labors. At the same time, it invites any interested party to reflect upon the reservoir of human gifts that were channeled through the mission of Mount Angel over almost 140 years. It stands as a unique and still active example of the durability of monastic tradition and the fruitfulness of its presence.

Index